S0-BFE-287

MOVE IN OUR MIDST

Looking at
worship in
the life of
the church

KENNETH MORSE

THE BRETHREN PRESS

Copyright © 1977, The Brethren Press
Printed in the United States of America
Cover design by Wilbur E. Brumbaugh

Library of Congress Cataloging in Publication Data

Morse, Kenneth I.
  Move in our midst

    1. Liturgics—Church of the Brethren.
2. Liturgics. I. Title.
BX7825.M67   264'.06'5   77-6411
ISBN 0-87178-583-8

CONTENTS

Move in our midst, Thou Spirit of God;
  Go with us down from Thy holy hill;
Walk with us through the storm and the calm;
  Spirit of God, go Thou with us still.

Touch Thou our hands to lead us aright;
  Guide us forever; show us Thy way.
Transform our darkness into Thy light;
  Spirit of God, lead Thou us today.

KM, 1941

Foreword

In September of 1974, a group of eight persons met in a farmhouse retreat setting to think about worship in the life of the Church of the Brethren. Among the participants were artists, musicians, writers, pastors, and teachers. They shared some common concerns such as:

—Concern for deepening the quality and meaning of corporate worship experiences in the local church.

—Concern for integrity between life experiences and the forms and language of worship.

—Concern for lay involvement and use of the gifts of members in worship experiences.

—Concern for a better understanding of the meaning and purpose of worship in the life of our church.

The retreat bore fruit. From that experience came a proposal for a major Parish Ministries Commission emphasis in the area of worship resources. The proposal included three publications, (1) a new "Pastor's Manual," (2) a new worship resources workbook for congregational use, and (3) a thirteen-week study unit on worship in the life of the church. The Commission approved the proposal in October of 1974.

Move in Our Midst is the thirteen-week study unit. Its style and content will allow it to be used privately for understanding and reflection, or in a group setting for study and discussion. Ken Morse's special gifts are clearly visible in this writing. His long interest in worship; his gifts in language, music, and art; his understanding of Christian symbols; his personal experiences in the church, here and abroad; and his sense of continuity between faith language and faith experience; all have served to make this a simple, yet profound and helpful resource. The Commission expresses its gratitude to Ken for his work, and hopes that as the church studies the meaning of worship, the Spirit of God may, indeed, move in our midst in new and invigorating ways.

Earle W. Fike, Jr., Executive
Parish Ministries Commission

1
For Us, the Living:
An Invitation to Worship

It is not the dead who praise the Lord,
not those who go down into silence;
but we, the living, bless the Lord,
now and for evermore. Ps. 115:17-18 (NEB)

"Come, let us worship." The invitations are out, and
your name is on the list. A recent writer, David J. Randolph, describes Christian worship as "a party for which
God is host and to which everyone is invited." That description may seem too lighthearted for persons who
regard worship as being in touch with the highest and the
holiest evidences of God's presence. But, however you
think of worship—with awe and wonder, with deep
awareness of your own limitations, with a feeling of joy
and celebration, or a mixture of all of these—its scope is
all inclusive.

Everyone is invited. Can you imagine the response
you would receive if you selected persons at random
from the phone book or as you met them on the street,
and said, "Come, let us worship"? Or even if you hedged
your chances by limiting your personal invitation to
members of your congregation? Here your task of ex-
plaining what worship involves would be easier, but even

so you would find a great difference in needs and expectations.

Do you, for example, know persons like these:

1. *Henry* is in his early sixties. He grew up on the farm, later moved to town. Life used to have a fairly orderly pattern for Henry, but lately he feels threatened: by strikes, robberies, taxes, pornography, new lifestyles—you name it, Henry's against it. Henry wants church services to be familiar: the "old" hymns, some quiet music, biblical preaching, not too many innovations. Henry has no theories about worship, but he can tell you what the preacher said—or failed to say.

2. *Sharon* is in her mid-thirties. She will quickly tell you how a newly liberated woman reacts in an old worship service. Sharon feels left out by the male language of readings and songs. Words like "Lord" and "king" only add to her frustration. It helps when women lead in worship, but most services cause Sharon to think she is "less than a full person."

3. *Joe* is in the eighth grade. He likes the outdoor, informal times of worship at weekend retreats or summer camp, but Sunday services seldom speak to him. So he chooses the back seat in the balcony or some place near the door. On occasions where there is a drama or a youth chorus or guitars, Joe feels involved. But he stumbles over readings from the bulletin, and some hymns sound like a foreign language. He can tell you how long the preacher spoke, but not what was said.

4. *J. Richard* always uses his first initial, but friends call him "Rich." He subscribes to symphony concerts, maintains an apartment furnished with excellent taste. He likes to have everything—including worship—carried out with "class." He takes some Bible readings and sermons the way he takes opera: the stories may seem childish, but the music or poetry impresses him. He likes "good" music, "good" decor; and he likes church—as long as he can be a detached critic of what he sees and hears.

5. *Jenny* is really with it when the music is loud and she is surrounded by it. Of college age, Jenny doesn't

care too much how or when things happen (she doesn't need a program) as long as they "happen." For Jenny, things do happen sometimes in worship, especially in the drama of the love feast or in celebration-type services. She likes banners and balloons, lively songs, short sermons, and, best of all, the sharing time when people really "tell it like it is."

6. *"Dutch"* has been a man about town for so long that no one can recall his real name. First a factory worker, then a sales rep, Dutch works and plays competitively, yielding to no one. His judgments are quick, yes or no, black or white. His tastes are on the corny side. For him the church should be the church, a place to support him but not to challenge what he does the rest of the week. He wants worship to be familiar, in his everyday language—and to end on time so he can prepare the backyard barbecue.

7. *Dan* would like to be called "brother" by everyone, especially when he is trying to restore the old Brethren ways. He is great for simple living, the rituals of feetwashing and the holy kiss, but he can hardly stand fancy music on the organ, fancy glass in the windows, the open chancel, or robes on the preacher or the choir. Printed bulletins and rehearsed prayers are sinful in his eyes, but he is happy when the message turns to service, sacrifice, discipleship, or the peace witness.

8. *Ruth* is quiet and withdrawn. Her tendency is to shrink back into herself when she is noticed, but church gatherings are terribly important for her. In some services Ruth is almost lost—she is made to feel less important than ever. But in others Ruth glimpses a new identity, and in spite of herself she is drawn into a warm and loving circle that lifts her out of her loneliness.

9. *Connie,* just turned five, thinks of church in terms of the faces of family and friends. Most of the words she ignores, but she never misses a greeting or a smile. A few songs puzzle her. A few belong to her. But mostly she draws pictures, fills in blank spaces on the bulletin, explores her mother's purse, or combs her father's beard. Yet the rituals of conversation tell Connie she belongs.

10. *Helen* is happiest when things are in order—as they have been during most of her fifty years. She likes to see evidence of structure in a worship service. She may not agree with every part, but it ought to make sense. Spontaneous responses—a shouted "amen" or an unplanned testimony—make her uneasy. Helen tries to be broadminded, but she often wonders why worship leaders don't have better control over what happens.

People are important
In beginning a study of worship it is essential to consider the needs and aspirations of people, as different or as difficult as each one of us may be. If you did not find yourself in the ten we described above, be sure to make your own list, beginning with a look at your own feelings and expectations when you respond to the call to "come and worship."

Given such a variety of individual preferences, not to mention the cultural differences you can find within one congregation, we may think it well-nigh impossible for people to gather at one time and in one place to worship. But God is not as limited in communicating love and grace to us as we are in understanding them. While we may begin by thinking just of ourselves, in any experience of worship we soon realize that God has been active through history and continues now to reach out to us, seeking us. Our need is to open our eyes, become aware of God's activity, and welcome our creator's presence into our hearts.

Can you describe worship?
How shall we define worship? Some good working definitions are available, but no one formulation can begin to describe all that worship means. For a definition that is comprehensive in its scope and beautifully phrased, suitable for framing in your memory, take these words by William Temple: *"To worship is to quicken the conscience by the holiness of God, to feed the mind with the truth of God, to purge the imagination by the beauty of God, to open the heart to the love of God, to devote*

will to the purpose of God."

Other dimensions of worship come into view with
more recent definitions. James F. White observes that
*"Christian worship is the deliberate act of seeking to ap-
proach reality at its deepest level by becoming aware of
God in and through Jesus Christ and by responding to
this awareness."*

However we define worship there are several
characteristics that must be emphasized, all of them
reflecting what the Bible adds to our understanding of
worship. Consider these aspects:

1. *Worship involves appreciation.* The origin of the
word worship makes it clear that it once meant "worth-
ship." It applied to deeds and attitudes that showed appreciation for the worth of a particular object or person.
In Christian worship we recognize God as one worthy of
our appreciation, before whom we bow down or
otherwise show our respect. We can identify with the awe
expressed in Psalm 8. The psalmist is overwhelmed by
the glory of God's creation and therefore comes to a new
appreciation both of the worth of God and of human
responsibility. We can join our songs with those, in the
Revelation of John (4:9-11), who cast down their crowns
and cry out to God, "Worthy art thou . . . to receive
glory and honor and power." Or like Isaiah, we may
move from our appreciation of God's glory and goodness
to recognize our own limitations and our need for cleaning (Isa. 6:1-5).

2. *Worship involves an expectant heart.* What matters
is not a particular time or place or the observance of
time-honored ceremonies, but the real hunger of the
human spirit to be in touch with God's spirit. Jesus came
close to defining true worship in his conversation with a
Samaritan woman. He shifted her attention away from
arguments about where and how to worship and urged
her to see that God, being Spirit, seeks worshipers who
come "in spirit and in truth." This particular insight
regarding the reality of worship also affirms the expectancy of God, picturing God as one who is seeking true
worshipers who will come "in spirit and in truth." (John

4:19-24). In such spiritual worship we can begin to realize who God is and who we are. That awareness should lead us also to see others as persons for whom Christ died and therefore as having value in God's sight.

3. *Worship involves the offering of ourselves* as well as the sharing of our possessions. Most expressions of worship in pagan and ancient practices as well as in Christian services, have included some form of sacrifice or offering. A familiar passage from the Old Testament (Deut. 26:1-11) indicates how Hebrew worshipers were expected to bring an offering of the "first fruits" of their harvest and along with it to offer a confession of faith and words of thanksgiving. The early Christians, no longer bound to a system of animal sacrifice and burnt offerings, still brought their contributions to their services, at first holding their possessions in common.

But true worship requires more than token offerings by way of material gifts. Our response to God is prompted by the magnitude of divine grace as personified in Jesus Christ. We love God because God first loved us. "If God so loved us, we ought to love one another" (1 John 4:11). Because Jesus was sent to make God's love known, we are encouraged, like Isaiah, to say "Here am I, send me." In this connection note how Paul relates worship to the offering of a living sacrifice in Rom. 12:1. Two familiar translations and a new Brethren one can be quoted. In the Revised Standard Version the verse reads: "I appeal to you therefore, brethren, by the mercies of God to present your bodies as a living sacrifice, holy and acceptable to God, which is your *spiritual worship.*" The New English Bible reads: "Therefore, my brothers, I implore you by God's mercy to offer your very selves to him: a living sacrifice, dedicated and fit for his acceptance, *the worship offered by mind and heart.*" And Graydon Snyder's "Believers New Testament" version puts it this way, "Be willing in your relationship to each other to place yourself on the altar as a living sacrifice, which is a life set apart for God and well pleasing to him. That would be worship in the truest sense of the word."

4. *Worship involves communion.* Someone has recently suggested that what we call worship might well be described as a meeting, a meeting of persons with God and a meeting with our brothers and sisters. This may simply be another way of emphasizing the communion aspect of worship. "Where two or three are gathered" in Jesus' name, we have the assurance of God's presence with them. Surely the assembling of believers, in the earliest Christian services, was understood as an evidence of Christ's body. For them the real presence of Christ was not limited to some mystical character of the Lord's Supper, even though that could appropriately be regarded as "communion" in the deepest spiritual sense. Some Christians regard every experience of worship as an evidence of the presence of God among us—in our midst, here and now, an event that calls forth joy and thanksgiving.

To aid our preparation for worship

This study book has been prepared for persons who want to respond to the invitation to "come and worship." Its pages are directed primarily to lay members of congregations in the Church of the Brethren who will not be satisfied merely to attend services of worship but who will also accept a measure of responsibility for what happens in worship. To worship in spirit and in truth calls for more than simply being present in body while someone else "leads" or functions in a priestly or ministerial way. As these pages will demonstrate, all Christians are called to accept a vocation in worship. Even if there is need for a set-apart ministry in the life of a congregation, the participation of every member in a "priesthood of all believers" is central in Christian worship, particularly as understood by the Church of the Brethren from its beginnings.

But we cannot participate in truly meaningful worship unless we are informed as to its character and purposes. Too often in the Church of the Brethren, since we have not emphasized a particular liturgical tradition and may have seemed to oppose many liturgical practices, instruction in worship participation has been minimal or lacking altogether. As a result we have frequently lost sight of the heritage of congregational responsibility for worship that once marked our Brethren ways. And this can be doubly disastrous if we also lose sight of the biblical teachings, by way of precept and example, that should undergird and illuminate our practices.

For these reasons this study includes a look at Hebrew worship and at the developments that characterized worship in the New Testament church. The study also underlines values in many of the worship traditions that have developed through the centuries since the time of Jesus. But primary attention is focused on the forms of worship that grow out of the free church tradition, with special emphasis on distinguishing practices among Brethren and with a look at Brethren convictions regarding worship. Hopefully, by learning more about our own heritage, by examining the rituals that Brethren have cherished as well as the concerns that support them, we may be better able to appropriate similar values— along with specific practices—and incorporate them intelligently into our worship today.

In many churches, including those whose traditions have been most rigid and formal, there is evidence today of new interest in worship patterns, an eagerness to experiment with new forms, and a hunger for more reality and integrity in worship. Brethren worshipers are sometimes handicapped in dealing with such innovations because we do not always understand the old forms that the new forms seek to renew or replace. All of this adds up to a need for even a brief survey of worship practices and some acquaintance with the rich heritage that art and music and language contribute to worship usages.

Only as we are better informed regarding some terms and practices that may seem strange to us can we expect to be able to select and adapt—and, in some cases, to reject—proposals that seek to renew and revitalize worship. (A glossary of terms, including many that may sound strange to Brethren ears, has been included for handy reference.) We need to be open to new insights from Bible study and from learning about our own and other traditions. In such a manner we can join with our neighbors in ecumenical worship and, hopefully, be prepared to interpret and share the Brethren practices that seem to be especially appropriate today.

Worship is the work of every participating member in a congregation, but it is also a delight and a joy for every child of God. Your name is on the invitation list. And the work is in your hands.

2
Look to the Rock:
Our Hebrew Heritage

Look to the rock from which you were hewn,
and to the quarry from which you were digged.
Isa. 51:1 (RSV)

If you could stand today in Jerusalem where Jewish worshipers still come to pray before their "wailing wall," you would marvel at its massive stones solidly placed, one row on top of another, to a height of almost 60 feet. This is all that remains after nineteen hundred years and a few more since Herod's temple stood there, the temple that Jesus visited as a boy, where he argued with learned doctors, and where he drove out the moneychangers.

But perhaps you would marvel even more at what the temple has signified for Jewish worshipers for almost three thousand years. Here it was that David chose a threshing floor overlooking his capital city as a suitable place for a national shrine. Here it was that Solomon brought builders and craftspeople from various countries to erect the first temple. After its destruction in the sixth century and following long years of captivity in Babylon, a second temple replaced it. But that too was destroyed, and centuries later Herod the Great must build it again. Now all that remains of Herod's great temple is a portion of the retaining wall, a memorial of past glories. But even now it is a setting for worship when Jews return to their homeland and recall the earlier temples they associated with God's presence.

A faith that can survive for thousands of years without being crushed by the rise and fall of empires must have qualities that are far more durable than stones. It is to these qualities that we turn when we look for characteristics of Hebrew worship. Christians still share some of these characteristics, even though today our customs and ceremonies differ greatly from the activities that were once the center of attention in Jerusalem. We have no need for an elaborate system of offerings and sacrifices to bring us close to the "holy of holies" where God dwells. Rather we celebrate our conviction that God has come to us in Jesus Christ and that the tabernacle of God is with the persons who love and serve God, wherever they happen to be. Yet we still need to appreciate what it must have meant to Jews to visit their temple on one of their great festival days.

Temple worship: A processional for pilgrims
Try to imagine, if you can, the feeling of excitement and the sense of anticipation Hebrew worshipers must have experienced when they joined a procession moving toward the Jerusalem temple. Many of them, especially those who lived some distance from the city, could not attend regular Sabbath services. But there were annual festivals when everyone was expected to make the pilgrimage to the holy city, as did the family of Jesus when he was a boy.

There were special songs for the pilgrims to sing, some of which are included in the book of Psalms (120-134). Also there were processional hymns that seemed to be created especially for the moments when the worshipers would stand before the gates of the temple waiting for the doors to open. Psalm 24 is such a hymn. You may be standing with your family just outside the raised temple area. You become alert when robed priests enter the area carrying the ark. Also in the procession are singers and musicians playing instruments, other priests, and many more worshipers waiting to enter.

The psalm begins with a hymn of praise (vs 1-2) to God who is far more than a local or national deity. God is the one to whom heaven and Earth belong. All the fulness of the world and its inhabitants are God's. The creator of the universe, no less, is the one whom the worshipers are approaching.

Then a challenging voice, perhaps that of a priest, asks a startling question (v. 3). Who, indeed, is worthy to approach the heights on which the temple stands? Who can enter the holy place where God dwells? An answering voice spells out the requirements (vs. 4-6): clean hands, pure heart, a life of moral uprightness. The temple will surely receive those whose eager faces are turned toward the God of Jacob.

Now the crowd of seekers waits at the temple doors. They address their song of praise to the holy gates, asking that they be opened to the King of glory (vs. 7). Their entrance hymn applies not only to themselves as pilgrims but also to the coming of God to be present with them. A solo voice (v. 8) asks them to identify and describe the God they await. In this particular hymn, they picture a leader in battle, a Lord of hosts, strong and mighty.

As the procession continues, the antiphonal voices are heard again, asking the same question, receiving almost the same answer (vs. 9-10). Some scholars think this was part of a much older liturgy, recalling the time when the ark was first carried in a dramatic way into the city of Jerusalem (2 Sam. 6:12-19). If this should be true, it reminds us that the ceremony of a processional, like many other common worship practices, is of ancient origin.

A vision, a call—and what God requires
To get some sense of what it must have been like to worship within the temple, listen to the prophet Isaiah when he explains the occasion of God's call to him and the setting in which he sensed the presence of God as well as the voice speaking directly to him (Isa. 6:1-8). It was a

year to remember, perhaps a time of national uncertainty, if not a time of crisis: the year King Uzziah died. So many aspects of temple worship could contribute to the experience of an impressionable young man. As he listened to the singing and chanting of the temple service, one voice calling to another and joining in a hymn to the holiness of God, the whole atmosphere called to his mind the majesty and glory as well as the goodness of God.

What Isaiah saw and heard and felt at that time spoke to his heart, so that he cried out in awareness of his sin, perhaps comparing his weakness to the power of God and his uncleanness to the goodness of God. Yet, for Isaiah, the words that he heard in the temple spoke to him also of God's forgiveness and healing. And the gift that he received from the altar provided the cleansing he needed and the assurance of his acceptance by God.

But there was still another dimension to his vision. Isaiah understood that God was asking for something more than a burnt offering or participation in a ceremony. He sensed that God was asking for the commitment of his life in prophetic service. The experience of Isaiah in the temple was not complete until he personally was moved to respond and to say, "Here am I, send me."

Even as you ponder the depth and intensity of Isaiah's temple experience, and even as you acknowledge that many others must have been stirred in the same way, you will want to weigh seriously the witness of some other prophets who questioned the superficial character of much that passed for worship in the temple. Note particularly the words of Amos (Amos 5:21-24), who seriously doubted whether God was interested in the odor of burnt sacrifices or even in the melody of harps in the midst of solemn assemblies, when both justice and righteousness were lacking in the nation. Consider the prophetic witness of Jeremiah (Jeremiah 7:21-26), who suggested that God was more interested in obedience than in burnt offerings. And note also how the prophet Micah (Micah 6:6-8) affirms that what the Lord requires is "to do justice and to love mercy, and to walk humbly with your God."

The hymnbook of the temple

Though many things about the Jerusalem temple would strike us as alien to our own worshiping, certainly if we could listen with understanding to the actual wording of its songs and hymns, we would discover that they are already familiar to our ears. The book of Psalms is likely that portion of the Old Testament we know best of all, especially in the context of worship. This "Hymnbook of the Second Temple," as the psalter has been described, is a collection of 150 religious poems intended both for private and public use. Though these songs and hymns come from many periods of Israel's history, they were probably compiled in their present arrangement between 400 and 200 BC.

Many of the psalms were intended to be sung or chanted to the accompaniment of musical instruments; and at least one psalm (150) calls on all such sources of music to praise the Lord.

You may not be aware of how often you draw on the resources of the "Hymnbook of the Temple" in your own worship until you note particularly how many of the hymns you love come from the Hebrew psalms. If you look in your hymnal at the index of authors, translators, and sources of words, you will note that quite a few hymns come directly from the psalms. But even this listing is not complete because many of our standard hymns come from the days when Christians sang metrical arrangements of the Hebrew psalms. Many hymnwriters, even without feeling the need to give special recognition to their source, quoted actual phrases as well as using the basic concepts of Hebrew songs of praise. Look also at the index of scriptural allusions that your hymnal provides. *The Brethren Hymnal,* for example, indicates that more than half of the 150 psalms are reflected more or less directly in its pages.

Long after the temples were destroyed, when Jews who were scattered throughout the Roman world gathered in synagogues for worship, they continued to sing the psalms that they loved. And Christians too. There are 93 quotations from the psalms in the New Testament. As churches developed their own worship patterns they preserved the Hebrew songs of praise, either by quoting them directly in their liturgies, or by adapting them for use as hymns.

A song of hallelujah

The contribution of the Hebrew temple to our worship can be illustrated by looking in more detail at two psalms, among many that might be chosen. Psalm 148 is one of five great hallelujah songs at the end of the psalter. It offers a call to the entire universe to praise God, beginning with a summons to heavenly creation (angels, hosts, sun, moon, stars) and following with an invitation to Earthly creation (fire, hail, snow, mountains, trees, cattle, birds, kings, and ordinary people) to join in praising God. This is the psalm that St. Francis had in mind when he wrote his lovely "Canticle to the Sun" in the 13th century. But it also appears in different form, yet with some of the same imagery and the same invitation to praise, in a hymn we love, "All Creatures of Our God and King."

Perhaps you are better acquainted with Psalm 103, an individual song of thanksgiving. There is a tradition that identifies this as the hymn that Jesus and his disciples sang at the conclusion of the Last Supper. Certainly it was a popular one among Jewish and Christian worshipers. It has come into our services for worship not only as an appropriate reading, but also in the hymn by James Montgomery, "O Bless the Lord My Soul." It is one of several hymns set to quite modern music in the popular musical "Godspell." A modern setting for the psalm is offered in *The Brethren Songbook* (No. 1.) But however and whenever we hear or sing it, the text affirms the mercy of God as a loving parent who remembers and forgives.

Synagogue worship

Despite the affection that many Jews felt for their temple in Jerusalem (still reflected in the devotion of worshipers who cherish their visits to the "wailing wall") they learned how to continue their religious practices after the temple was destroyed. Both in Palestine and in communities to which they were scattered, they came together in synagogues regularly for worship and instruction. Some synagogues were impressive buildings, but many were simple, serving the religious needs of a small number of Jewish worshipers. There was no provision for sacrifices and no need for priests. The building would provide a raised platform and a chest containing the scrolls of the Law and the Prophets. Though many synagogues developed during Old Testament times, they are not mentioned there but they are frequently referred to in the New Testament.

Luke's gospel tells us in some detail about a particular synagogue. What better occasion for a visit than the service in Nazareth on an occasion when Jesus attended—and spoke (Luke 4:14-30). Although there was no printed bulletin, the service followed an outline something like this: the recitation of the Shema (Deut. 6:4 and following); a prayer; a fixed reading from the Law; a free reading from the Prophets; an explanation of one of the Scripture readings; and a blessing or a prayer. Psalms were also sung. There was no official minister or priest, although the men of the congregation would elect a president to see that the traditions were followed. A lay member or a visitor (but not a woman) could read and comment on the reading.

There was a simple kind of ritual associated with the synagogue service, as Luke indicates in his narrative. Services were held on the Sabbath day. The worshipers lived in one community (tradition said that any ten men of good character could form a congregation), and the "custom" of regular attendance was encouraged. Jesus followed their practice of standing to read, sitting to preach. Since the reading from the prophets was optional, he selected an appropriate passage from the Isaiah scroll. Then he announced, as he began to apply the message to his day and to himself, that the mission described by the prophet was to be his mission. What happened later might also reflect the informality of a synagogue service, but the violent reaction to Jesus was prompted by his message and was certainly not a common experience. As will be noted in later chapters, out of the synagogue services came many of the worship forms that were adopted by the earliest Christian churches, including practices that are common today.

Frequently we look for worship resources outside the Bible that we feel can enrich our services. If you wish particularly to celebrate the common heritage that Christians share with devout Jews, it would be appropriate to examine the prayers and hymns currently used in Jewish homes and in their synagogue services. Many of these extol the one God of the universe but who is also loving and compassionate and concerned for the entire creation.

For example, many Jewish worshipers repeat a prayer known as the Eighteen Benedictions, which includes these words of thanksgiving to God:

"We will give thanks unto thee
And declare thy praise
For our lives which are committed unto thy hand,
And for our souls which are in thy charge,
And for thy miracles which are daily with us,
And for thy wonders and thy benefits
Which are wrought at all times,
Evening, morn and noon."

There is one Hebrew hymn that we frequently sing, a hymn that derives not from the psalms but rather from the efforts of a Jewish philosopher to bring together the fundamental principles of Judaism. His name was Moses Maimonides, a Spanish Jew who lived in the 12th century. His formulation of principles of the faith, which may be the nearest thing to a creed that Jewish worshipers have, was recast in the form of a hymn by Daniel ben Judah around the year 1300 in Rome. The hymn appears in many Christian hymnals under the title "The God of Abraham Praise" (No. 38, *The Brethren Hymnal*) and is used there with an arrangement of a Hebrew melody. It is a hymn that is appropriate for any occasion that calls for adoration and praise not only to the God of Abraham but to the God of us all.

3
After the Manner of Christ: New Testament Patterns

Agree with one another after the manner of Christ Jesus, so that with one mind and one voice you may praise the God and Father of our Lord Jesus Christ.
Rom. 15:5-6 (NEB)

Almost everyone has wished for a time machine—a contraption that could spin you to a place you would like to visit and put you in the midst of events at some decisive moment in history. Just as there are times you would like to live through again, so there are times and places you would schedule for a close examination—if you could.

Take the events associated with the life of Jesus and the beginnings of the Christian church. Suppose with one gauge on your time machine you could select Palestine, with another the first century. Could you not learn much more about worship "after the manner of Christ" if you could sit with the multitudes who first heard the Sermon on the Mount or those who watched Jesus "cleanse" the temple? Or would you elect to be in a Christian assembly in a believer's home in Jerusalem right after the day of Pentecost? How about attending church in Corinth on the exact day when the leaders of the congregation read a letter from Paul?

Unfortunately you cannot move backward in time; even if you could, you might well be advised that you travel at your own risk in casting your lot—even as an observer—with the minority group of first-century Christians. But still, for those of us who are curious about worship in early Christian times, there are enough scattered references, and even simple descriptions of services, in the New Testament to help us grasp some of their basic characteristics. We have already noted Luke's vivid description of Jesus's part in a synagogue service. From both his teaching and his example we can learn how he must have felt about many of the worship practices of his day.

Jesus' teaching and example

Whatever personal feelings Jesus may have had about the ceremonies that were observed in the temple and in the synagogues, he did not directly attack them or condemn them. Instead of questioning specific practices he was most concerned about the sincerity and honesty of the worshipers, lest they become enamored of the public display of their piety and forget the purpose of prayer (Look especially at Matt. 6:1-19). Jesus was most critical of the motives of persons who made a show of their worship and thereby lost sight of its proper focus.

So he offered surprising and sometimes shocking proposals: in giving alms to help others, Jesus' followers were to keep the details of their generosity secret. Secrecy in prayer would also be a guard against public hypocrisy. The important thing was the modest integrity of a prayer, not its length or phrasing. And when they fasted, they were not to pretend to suffer (for the sake of public attention) but rather to celebrate with a spirit of joy. Yet in all these teachings, while it might seem that Jesus was encouraging devout Jews to turn away from their worship practices, he made clear his purpose—"not to destroy, but to fulfill"—as if to say that ceremonies and practices can become hollow and meaningless if they are followed without understanding in the spirit of true worship.

You are probably familiar with the various accounts of Jesus' cleansing the temple (Matt. 21:12-17; Mark 11:15-18; Luke 19:45-48; John 2:13-17). Many greedy practices had come to be associated with temple worship—to the extent that the area provided for prayer by Gentiles had become a noisy place of trade. In protesting against such obvious evils as he saw there, Jesus may have appeared to threaten the temple system, but his purpose was really to cleanse and reform, and by such direct action to remind everyone that the temple was intended as a house of prayer for all nations. We know that Jesus attended temple services just as he went, "as his custom was" to the synagogue. So it is not surprising that his followers carried over into Christian worship many Jewish practices or that the great devotional texts of the Old Testament were important in their literature and in their liturgy. But, thanks to his teaching, his dynamic ministry, and the significance of his life and death and resurrection, something new had been added; a new spirit, a new power, a new reason for rejoicing and praising God.

Day by Day in Jerusalem
Because the first Christians who met together for worship after the resurrection were Jews, we should not be surprised to learn that they kept many of the customs of the synagogue. Again it is Luke who tells us about some of the earliest gatherings. He doesn't exactly provide us with an order of worship, but from such passages as Acts 2:42-46; 4:23-31; 5:42; and 6:2-4 we learn that these Jerusalem Christians not only went to the temple but worshiped in homes. That assembling for worship was not only weekly but daily. That they prayed together often (one of the earliest prayers appears in Acts 4:24-30). That they ate together in love feasts that strengthened their fellowship. That they celebrated the Lord's Supper. That their teaching and preaching affirmed that Jesus was Lord. And that in all their observances they praised God, whose word they wanted to speak with boldness.

One way of describing the changes in worship that developed when Jews first became Christians is to say that the Upper Room was added to the synagogue. What was distinctively Christian at first was the recognition that the expected Messiah had indeed come and that his followers now, even though they sang many of the familiar psalms and read the old Scriptures, would now affirm the life and death and resurrection of Jesus and would seek to follow in their own ritual the simple instructions he gave them at the Lord's Supper.

Sunday meetings in Corinth

But soon there were Christians who were not Jews, there were churches away from Jerusalem, and there were new messages to hear, new witnesses to listen to, new problems to face. How would this affect the shape of Christian worship?

The letters of Paul are no more helpful than are the narratives of Luke in providing a specific outline of worship. But again there are hints as to practices that were followed. We have Paul's own suggestions as to what worship should include, and we are privileged to see how Paul dealt with problems related to worship in the Corinthian church.

First of all, there was a new day for congregational worship. The first day of the week came to be known as the Lord's Day because it was the day of resurrection and also the day when the power of the Holy Spirit became apparent at Pentecost. On this day Christians would assemble, likely in homes, in order to teach the word of Christ, admonish one another and sing "psalms and hymns and spiritual songs with thanksgiving" to God.

We know from Paul's letters that offerings were an important element in the congregation's weekly meetings and that he had authorized "the collection for the saints," often as a way to help with very specific needs. We are still urged to give in the spirit of the Macedonian Christians whose example Paul describes in 2 Corinthians, an example of voluntary giving out of abundance, not as one would pay a tax or fulfill an obligation but from the joy of sharing in the ministry of Christ.

It seems apparent, from Paul's words, that members of a congregation were encouraged to share in the development of the worship service, perhaps offering a hymn or song, perhaps giving a testimony or an exhortation for the benefit of other members. But this was the area in which the Corinthian church ran into difficulties. And the list of troublesome issues in the church there that came to Paul's attention included the question of leadership, especially where spiritual gifts were concerned.

Paul is especially helpful when he deals with worship problems in the Corinthian church. He doesn't lay down any hard rules, and he tries to be sensitive to the individual gifts that worshipers want to share, yet he thinks "all things should be done decently and in order." To the first-century charismatics who must have caused some confusion in Corinth, Paul speaks of a more excellent way, the way of love. While he appreciates the value of spiritual gifts that can catch up a worshiper into an ecstatic trance, he counsels all worshipers to guard against "doing your own thing" to the extent that it interferes with the well-being of the whole body. And to the persons who rushed into the love feast meal, thinking only of themselves and forgetting others, he urges them to "discern the body" and to "wait for one another."

While the freedom of expression that was evident in the Corinthian church had many good qualities—the gifts were indeed spiritual—Paul pointed out the danger of excess. Some individual expressions must be restrained for the benefit of the whole body. So Paul urged worshipers to sing with the mind as well as the spirit—good counsel for singers in every generation.

Songs old and new

What kind of songs did they sing? Christian singers surely used the familiar Psalter, the song book of the Hebrew temple, but they were also learning other hymns and songs. Unfortunately for those of us who are curious about such things we do not know what hymns Paul and

Silas sang in prison at Philippi (Acts 16:25). But we do
know that other prisoners listened. Neither can we be
sure of the distinctions, if any, Paul made between
"hymns and spiritual songs" (Eph. 5:18-20). But we
can appreciate the spirit of praise and thanksgiving that
comes with "making melody to the Lord with all your
heart."

There are three nativity hymns that Luke included in
his narratives concerning the births of John the Baptist
and of Jesus. Many scholars believe that such hymns,
which resemble in form and language the psalms of the
Old Testament, were commonly sung in Christian
churches in the first century. Modern translations of
Luke's gospel present these hymns as poetry. Look first
at Luke 1:46-55, Mary's song of praise on the occasion of
her visit to Elizabeth. The "Magnificat," as it is called
from the Latin translation of its beginning, resembles the
song of Hannah, who also rejoiced in the promise of a
son. Mary glorifies God for what God has done and is
about to do. Her exclamation is more than a personal
cry of thanksgiving and wonder. It is really a
revolutionary reminder that the Messiah will scatter the
proud, put down the mighty and exalt the lowly. If such
a song was indeed a part of early Christian worship it
was more than an act of devotion. It was a fitting hymn
for a young movement that might some day "turn the
world upside down."

The two additional nativity hymns, though never as
popular as the Magnificat, also found a place in early
Christian services. They are the "Benedictus," (Luke
1:67-79), a song of praise to God spoken by Zechariah,
the father of John the Baptist, and the "Nunc Dimittis"
(Luke 2:29-32), a short but eloquent hymn in the words
of Simeon, the old man who had looked for the coming
of the Messiah and who at last can hold the child Jesus
in his arms. Also appearing in early liturgies, it is still
used effectively on special occasions as a benediction.

Are there other hymns in the New Testament? Some
scholars believe that New Testament writers may have
quoted certain confessions of faith or ascriptions of

praise to Christ that were either spoken or sung in unison by believers. One passage that seems to be liturgical in content and form is 2 Tim. 2:11-13. Obviously some of the triumphal songs in the book of Revelation (Rev. 4:8-11; Rev. 5:9-10; Rev. 15:3-4; and Rev. 19:1-8) have the character of a "hallelujah chorus" and they have found their way into hymns and oratorios. There are at least two familiar passages in Paul's letters that have the quality of early hymns. One would suspect that they early found a place in services of public worship. They are Phil. 2:5-11, surely a profound confession of faith, and Colossians 1:15-20, a magnificent and poetic expression of praise for Christ, "the image of the invisible God."

The memorial meal

We have already noted the references in Acts to the very frequent occasions when Christians ate together. This occasion from the beginning represented far more than the traditional Jewish practice of gathering for family or communal meals. And it just as surely signified something far deeper than a casual assembling for a church dinner. There are several indications in the New Testament that the simple act of breaking bread together carried for the first Christians a meaningful symbolism.

Look at what Paul wrote to the Corinthian church about their eating together (1 Cor. 11:17-34). It is clear that it was their practice to assemble as a church, yet by the time Paul was writing they were in danger of losing sight of the original purpose for such a time of meeting. He is referring to the agape meal, the sharing in a love feast for which they each brought food, that also included partaking of the bread and the cup that represented the body and the blood of Christ. Though we regret the problems (of selfishness and divisiveness) that made it necessary for Paul to write, we are grateful not only for his counsel to the Corinthians but for his giving us so explicit a statement regarding the Lord's Supper.

As we noted earlier, it was the experience of the Upper Room, translated into a frequent, recurring ritual for Christians, that became the unique contribution of early

Christian worship. In words of his own that recall the gospel accounts of what Jesus did and said in the Upper Room, Paul clearly sets forth the actions and the words of Jesus that are basic to our observance. The bread and the cup are still shared after the manner of Christ, who instructed us to "do this as a memorial of me." So we join in proclaiming "the Lord's death until he comes."

Second-century services
Apart from the New Testament there are other early Christian writings that describe congregational services. For example, the *Didache* (or Teaching), written early in the second century, contains a manual of church order with instructions for administering baptism, for fasting and prayer, and for conducting the communion, including prayers for the bread and the cup and a concluding prayer of thanksgiving. The writer says, "On every Lord's Day . . . come together and break bread and give thanks, first confessing your sins so that your sacrifice may be pure."

A little later in the same century a great apologist for the Christian faith, Justin, known as the Martyr, in his first *Apology* wrote, "And on the day called Sunday there is a meeting in one place of those who live in cities or the country, and the memoirs of the apostles or the writings of the prophets are read as long as time permits. When the reader has finished, the president in a discourse urges and invites (us) to the imitation of these noble things. Then we all stand up together and offer prayers . . . when we have finished the prayer, bread is brought, and wine and water."

Before long the simple congregational services developed into elaborate liturgies, becoming more formal, less spontaneous, and requiring the leadership of professional clergy. But the pattern for later liturgies was already developing. Two values are predominant: "the liturgy of the Word," meaning the readings and prayers and teaching that came from the synagogue, and "the liturgy of the Table," meaning the communion ceremonies instituted by Jesus in the Upper Room.

4
Varieties of Service:
A Look at Worship Traditions

There are varieties of gifts, but the same Spirit; and there are varieties of service, but the same Lord; and there are varieties of working but it is the same God who inspires them all in every one. 1 Cor. 12:4-6 (RSV)

The ways that Christians worship are almost as diverse as the churches in which they gather. Even within a particular tradition or among several churches of the same denomination we expect to find varied forms of worship. While we cannot expect to distinguish all of them or to classify them easily, we shall attempt to look briefly at several of the major worship traditions that are still followed by Christians today. Even a superficial survey may help us to appreciate their diversity and also recognize the contributions they all make to the service of the same God.

Although most traditions base their practices on biblical precedents, seeking in one way or another to worship after the manner of Christ, no doubt the earliest continuing traditions belong to churches we call Eastern Orthodox.

Eastern Orthodox worship

Come with me to the Russian Orthodox Church of St. Sergius, a modest brick building hidden away on a hillside in Paris. It is time for the annual Easter vigil which begins late on Saturday night and continues into the early hours of Easter morning. It is the climax of the Christian year for Eastern Orthodox Christians whether they live in Eastern countries, in Europe, or in the United States.

To a non-Orthodox visitor the most imposing aspect of an Orthodox church is likely to be the screen which covers the front of the church. It is called an *iconostasis* because it is composed of icons arranged in tiers. In an Orthodox church the iconostasis separates the sanctuary (the area that would correspond to the chancel) from the rest of the church. There are three doors, which permit the priests and deacons to move back and forth between the altar in the sanctuary and the worshiping congregation.

At the center of Orthodox life is the liturgy, the basic worship service of the church. It represents the gathering of the Lord's people on the Lord's day to break bread in a eucharistic meal. It is a time of thanksgiving. Although in the early years of the Christian church several different liturgies developed in Eastern churches, since the sixth century there are only two that are standard. One is the Liturgy of St. John Chrysostom, which is used on most Sundays, and the other is the Liturgy of St. Basil, which is celebrated in Lent and at the time of certain feasts.

At frequent intervals during each service a priest or deacon may move throughout the church with a censer filled with burning incense, so that the entire church will be filled with its fragrance. This is a mark of reverence representing the presence of Christ within the church and also among the worshipers. But if your sight is attracted by candlelight reflected on icons and your sense of smell by the burning of incense, the impression upon your ears is just as vivid. For the service demands almost continuous singing. The priest intones the invitations and prayers and instructions that tie the various parts together. He and his assistants chant antiphonally with the choir the various litanies. And the choir, composed entirely of boys and men singing always without accompaniment, offers ancient hymns in harmonic arrangements.

In describing the eucharist of the Orthodox churches, a German theologian, Dr. Ernst Benz, says that in its present form it differs little from the celebration of the primitive church. He compares it to "an elaborate, complicated mystery play." Certainly this is true if one pays attention to the dramatic manner in which the Orthodox in their Holy Week services recall and interpret important events associated with the death and resurrection of Christ.

All of these events of Holy Week, as well as the weeks of preparation before and during Lent, have anticipated the one, great, happy occasion of Eastertime, which for the Orthodox will begin a couple of hours before midnight on the Saturday before Easter. As the hour of midnight approaches all the worshipers hold candles but do not light them. For a few moments the other candles in the church are darkened. Then when the room is completely dark another procession forms and when all is ready all light their candles. Suddenly the church is alive with light.

Now the priest in charge says joyfully, "Christ is risen!" Other priests and deacons take up the refrain. And the people respond, "He is risen indeed!" At the same time the bells outside ring out to fill the whole neighborhood with a joyful sound. The music of the resurrection hymn is repeated. As the priest continues the ancient liturgy of the Eastern churches, he will raise up a candelabrum with three burning candles, and again affirm that "Christ is risen!" And with every proclamation of that fact, the congregation responds, "He is risen indeed!"

Before any worshipers leave they must further show their joy in the resurrection by exchanging a holy salutation (a threefold kiss of greeting alternating from one side to another) with friends. The expressions of hap-

piness on the faces of the worshipers seem to light up
with a glow that reflects the candle flames on every side.

But whether the Orthodox Christians go now to their
homes or whether, as in the case of several of the leaders
of the church in Paris, they remain at the church to
gather around a table laden with food, they are now
ready to participate in an agape meal, a veritable love
feast.

For Eastern Orthodox Christians worship means the
offering of one's whole life to God. Worship is the
meetingplace of people and God in this world, a meeting
that should result in an explosion of joy and thanksgiving. Worship is at the center of their church life, and
liturgy is at the heart of worship. They regard a fixed
liturgical order as necessary for the continuity of their
tradition.

Are there not dangers in holding so rigidly to a fixed
liturgy? One Orthodox leader acknowledges the danger
of ritualism, when the service becomes an end in itself, a
spectacle with little contact with the inner life of
believers. Yet he hastens to add that there is a danger of
ignoring ceremonies, lest Christianity become only
moralism and believers forget to celebrate their faith in
Christ.

Roman Catholic worship

The central act of worship for Roman Catholics is the
Mass, which is interpreted as a reenactment of the Lord's
Supper. Although the main outlines of the service have
changed little since the third or fourth century, many
new elements have been added with the passing of the
years. But at the heart of all the readings, prayers,
blessings and symbolic movements is an ancient drama in
which Jesus' death on Calvary is presented each time the
mass is heard.

If you observe the mass you may notice that some
parts of the service differ little from aspects of other
Christian services, for there will be invitations to
worship, prayers and collects, readings from the Epistle
and the Gospel, perhaps a short sermon, the recitation of

the creed, and a benediction. But there are some important differences: you note the centrality of the altar, the specific roles that are assigned to those who direct the service, the significance of the vestments they wear. Until recently the mass was given only in Latin. Now it can be heard in English. Also in recent years several measures have been taken to increase the participation of the laity.

Three words may help us to appreciate specific values of the mass that Roman Catholics emphasize. One is the importance of *offering*. In early Christian days worshipers brought the bread and wine and water that would be used in celebrating the Lord's Supper. Today the offering, as in most churches, represents in a different way the offering of oneself through the giving of money or something that represents material sacrifice.

An even more important word is *consecration*. For Catholics this term refers specifically to the pronouncing of words by which the substance of the bread and the wine actually become at that moment and in that place the substance of the body and blood of Christ. The drama of this moment of "transubstantiation" is underlined by the ringing of bells as well as by repeating the words of Jesus, "This is my body."

The third word is *communion*. As part of the Roman mass Catholic worshipers who wish to receive communion come forward to the altar rail. The bread, now viewed as the Host, or the consecrated body of Christ, is placed on the tongues of communicants. For most Catholic worshipers this is now the extent of their participation in the communion, although in the Eastern church and even in Roman churches in the early centuries, the people could receive both the bread and the cup.

In contrast to Eastern Orthodox worship, western churches gave major attention to the sufferings of Christ and the sinfulness of those for whom he suffered. The cross and the crucifix took a central place in worship. The church building also tended to remove the sacred altar, and the priestly activities associated with it, further from the congregation. The services seemed to emphasize a sacrificial system that recalled some of the elaborate temple ceremonies of the Hebrews. And for individuals the emphasis was on confession and penance for sin and on works of merit that would be acceptable to God.

But in recent years many reforms and movements for renewal within the Roman church have brought about a greater involvement of lay people in worship and more joyful and enthusiastic expressions of praise and thanksgiving to God. Some of the most creative attempts to translate traditional forms into contemporary celebration have been initiated by Roman Catholic clergy and lay leaders. And the opportunities for ecumenical worship, though still limited, are increasing so that in some communities there are more and more occasions when Catholic and Protestant believers can freely worship together.

Lutheran worship

The Protestant Reformation brought about drastic changes in the way Christians worshiped, chiefly through efforts to recover the New Testament concept of the church as the people of God. The reformers in different ways insisted on the priesthood of all believers, with laity as well as clergy carrying responsibilities in ministering to one another.

For the people to participate fully it was necessary that the services in which they shared should be translated into their own language. Martin Luther did not want to give up the Roman mass but rather to adapt it so that it would no longer represent a continuing sacrifice but would instead open the way to hear and respond to the Word of God. So he first of all prepared his own Latin service, retaining portions of the Mass. Then he introduced a German Mass. The sermon had a larger place. There was more emphasis on scripture and more of an act of thanksgiving encouraging fellowship with Christ. But liturgical actions and ceremonies were still important for Luther.

Perhaps the greatest contribution of Luther to our worship today was his concern for congregational shar-

ing in church music. For him the priesthood of all
believers meant that all the people should sing. He encouraged the use of chorale tunes already known by the
people; but he also wanted children to learn music in
school. In cities there should be choral societies. He
liked part-singing and encouraged composition by
writing many new hymns and by his efforts to turn portions of the liturgy into hymns. Early in his fruitful
ministry he produced for the use of worshipers a hymnbook containing 23 hymns.

While Lutheran Sunday services today may seem a
little strange to persons who are not familiar with that
tradition, a worshiper with the aid of a hymnal and serv-
icebook can participate fully, especially if there is a printed bulletin to serve as guide. Though services will vary
among Lutheran churches, the following outline from a
Lenten Sunday service in a midwestern church may serve
as an example:

Prelude
Hymn: "The Church's One Foundation"
Confession of Sins
Introit (*sung by adult choir*)
Kyrie (*from Service book*)
Gloria in Excelsis (*Service book*)
Prayer of the Day (*from bulletin*)
Anthem (*adult choir*)
First Lesson (*from Genesis*)
Psalmody (*from bulletin*)
Second Lesson (*Romans*)
Gradual (*adult choir*)
Lenten Sentence (*from Service book*)
Gospel (*from Mark*)
Hymn: "Hail, Thou Once Despised Jesus"
Sermon
Apostle's Creed (*from Service book*)
Announcements
Offering
Offertory (*from Service book*)
Prayer of the Church (*from bulletin*)
Lord's Prayer
Hymn: "When I Survey the Wondrous Cross"
Benediction

Anglican-Episcopal worship

As cathedrals go, the one that also serves as a chapel for Christ Church College in Oxford, England, is one of the smallest. At a Sunday morning service in July we were seated in the choir, a good location from which to let your eyes trace the intricate designs of the fan vaulting in the ceiling. There were other distractions, but we gave our full attention to a woman preacher who happened also to be a doctor of philosophy but did not talk like one. Because the cathedral choir was on holiday we heard only a little choral music. The service was spoken rather than sung. You could follow it in the *Book of Common Prayer,* knowing that the service itself, in its basic pattern, would vary little as you moved from one Anglican or Episcopal church to another around the world.

At Oxford we kept hearing about the martyrs for whom a monument was raised in the city's center. One of the three men who were burned at the stake there in the middle of the 16th century was Thomas Cranmer, the one who was responsible, far more than any other, for the first *Book of Common Prayer.* He was quite familiar not only with the Roman Catholic liturgy formerly used in England but also with the reforms that Martin Luther had instigated. Like Luther he chose to have all services in the language of the people, in this case in English. Indeed the readings in the *Book of Common Prayer* are so well phrased, with cadences and rhythms that suggest the beauty to be realized a little later in the King James translation of the Bible, that they are freely used by worshipers who may never have entered an Episcopal church.

Episcopalians and others in the Anglican communion often insist that they are neither Catholic nor Protestant, and there is a sense in which their church serves as a bridge uniting sacramental and biblical emphases. Surely their prayer book, more than any other characteristic, has been a means of giving identity and continuity to worship over a period of several hundred years. Within the Anglican churches there are great variations in the attention given to ceremonies and customs. These range from the "high" church Anglo-Catholics who most resemble Roman Catholics in their attention to an elaborate ceremony, to "low" church evangelicals who tend more to emphasize preaching and a less formal ritual. But all churches are guided by what the prayer book prescribes, and this assures that the worshiping congregation will regularly hear generous selections from the Bible and will join in prayers of profound understanding and beauty.

Beautiful as the language in the *Book of Common Prayer* may be by literary standards, does it continue to speak to common people in the common speech of our own time? No, say some Episcopalians, who recently have engaged in debates about the language of their prayer book. Like other traditions, the Anglican communion faces the question of translating even so successful and lasting a treasure as its liturgy into contemporary speech. Otherwise it may fail in its original purpose of guiding a worshiping congregation in "common" prayer.

Presbyterian and Reformed Worship

In 1536 a young Frenchman, John Calvin, already recognized as a reformer and the author of a major work in theology, came to Geneva, Switzerland, to a city that was early associated with the Protestant Reformation and to a cathedral already converted to worship after the Reformed custom. For thirty years Calvin remained in Geneva to preach from the pulpit of St. Pierre and to teach the doctrines that are still emphasized in Presbyterian and Reformed churches around the world. According to one historian, in those thirty years, Geneva changed from a frivolous town to a city "where all was fire and prayer, study, labor, and austerity." Though the reports may be exaggerated, they do bear witness to the power of Calvin's preaching.

Some of the reforms that Calvin required in worship were regarded as drastic—even by other reformers. He opposed the use of an organ or choir, objected to part-singing, and would allow no hymns except metrical translations of the Psalms. He permitted no color or ornament and dispensed with ceremonial acts and gestures. He was eager to discard rituals and customs for which he could find no biblical sanction.

Calvin developed a liturgy for French-speaking congregations that began with a recognition of God's majesty and authority, accompanied by the confession of the worshiper's sin and a prayer for pardon. His emphasis on psalm-singing, though limiting from a musical standpoint, helped to make the scriptures familiar to the people. The psalters that developed in Switzerland, in England, in Scotland, and later in the American colonies, have helped to enrich our heritage of song. So have we benefitted from Calvin's insistence on reading and preaching the Word. He wanted his liturgy also to encourage frequent communion, but in this he was not as successful. He wanted to bring the proclamation of the Word together with simple observance of the sacraments so that, as one Reformed person put it, "the sacrament seals what the Word proclaims."

Many Presbyterian and Reformed churches, especially in this country, follow patterns of worship that seem to adapt rather easily to worship practices in the Church of the Brethren. But it was not always so, as one investigation into Brethren attitudes toward worship will show. This writer remembers a Sunday morning in 1958 when several Brethren worshiped in the Evangelical church in Schriesheim in Germany. We met in a church building that replaced an earlier Reformed church where Alexander Mack had been a member.

In the Schriesheim church the worshipers stand as they sing hymns that Mack may often have sung. There are many stanzas for most hymns in the present hymnbook, but the congregation does not sing them all. Although they sing in unison, the organ at the rear of the sanctuary adds the harmonies that accompany their singing.

In the front of the church is the altar on which there are candles and flowers and an open Bible. The pulpit to the left is high and must be reached by a stairway, which the pastor uses during the hymn before the sermon. His message is biblical, based this morning upon Psalm 23. Among the listening congregation are many women and some men as well as a number of children. The white caps of two deaconesses are evident also.

There were many reasons why, at the beginning of the 18th century, Alexander Mack would be at odds with a state church whose beliefs and practices he could not conscientiously follow, including aspects of Reformed worship. But in 1958 the worship patterns at least did not seem so strange. The pastor on that Sunday said, "Our forms of worship may differ but form is not as important as the substance of faith."

Free Church Worship
In the seventeenth and eighteenth centuries in Europe various groups of Christians began to protest against the established churches (many of which were organized by "protestants") whose forms of worship they could not conscientiously follow. These separatists were also called-dissenters or nonconformists because they refused to obey religious rules established and enforced by the governments under which they lived. The churches they formed were sometimes called "free" churches because among the freedoms they wanted for themselves was the liberty of departing from or rejecting entirely the prescribed liturgy or the order of worship required in the established churches.

In England the Puritan movement got its name from Christians who wanted to reform the English Prayer Book in the light of what they thought was a "pure" interpretation of the Bible. They also objected to the vestments worn by clergymen, and to certain ceremonies like kneeling to receive communion. They wanted prayers to be more extemporaneous, and they wanted sermons rather than short homilies. They encouraged the singing of hymns by congregations, using many new texts that expressed their devotion and their beliefs. Among those nonconformist groups were Baptists, Congregationalists, and Methodists. Since many of the colonists who came to America were seeking religious freedom, our churches have a background of worship in the free church tradition.

The Methodists, though originally seeking to remain loyal to the Church of England, from the beginning emphasized the singing of hymns and the use of informal worship practices in their early cottage prayer meetings and outdoor services. Perhaps the most radical expression of freedom in worship can be found in the services of the Society of Friends. Quaker worship has been distinguished by the rejection of most outward forms and signs. Many Quaker meetings follow a pattern of silence, allowing individuals as they may be led by the Spirit freely to voice their deep personal or social concerns. In silence the worshiping community "centers down" in quiet awareness of the presence of God. The community gathers for worship usually in a very simple meetinghouse, often without a pastor or worship director. Quakers traditionally did not favor music, yet one Quaker poet, John Greenleaf Whittier, is the author of hymn texts that many Christians love to sing. There are, even in the "unprogramed" Quaker services, still some elements of ritual, particularly when an elder worshiper takes the leadership to "break the silence." In this country there are certain Quaker groups with pastoral leadership who, while still encouraging silent worship, also provide for "programed" worship.

In 1958 a British Quaker described a series of worship services on a Sunday at Kassel House, then a center for Brethren work, attended by persons from the three historic peace churches. Richard K. Ullmann wrote about that occasion in this manner:

> It was the final event of a day of worshiping and praying together. In the morning we gathered for a Meeting for Worship after the manner of Friends; and it was a very good meeting, for which our hearts and minds had been well prepared by two days of thinking and working together on our common concerns. Before noon we gathered again for a simple Mennonite service singing some of their beautiful ancient hymns and listening to a searching,

yet quite unpretentious, exposition of a passage from the New Testament. Then, in the evening, we celebrated the Love Feast after the manner of the Brethren, beginning with a time of prayer and self-examination, following with the "forgotten sacrament" when one of us would kneel down and wash another's feet and then receive the same humble service from him till most of us had rendered and received it, and ending with the communal meal and the Supper.

The so-called "free" churches have often been drawn together more by their common concerns about issues than by similarities in their worship. Yet common to all such worship is a freedom from a set liturgy or a rigid ritual and a conviction that worship is the responsibility not just of clergy or designated worship leaders but of every person in the gathered community, in which Christ dwells.

5
Brethren at Worship: New Testament Examples

"For I have given you an example, that you should also do as I have done to you. . . . If you know these things, blessed are you if you do them." John 13:15, 17 (RSV)

Christmas day, 1723. It was an important day in the history of the Brethren in America; a day filled with happenings that illustrate graphically how certain worship practices have been at the center of the church's life from the beginning. We turn to a classic description of that day by Martin G. Brumbaugh, nationally known educator, a former governor of Pennsylvania, and a historian of the Brethren:

> There is an activity at Peter Becker's house in Germantown. The spindles are still; and the voice of praise is raised. Six persons, Martin Urner, his wife Catherine, Henry Landis, his wife, Frederick Lang, and John Mayle, all from what is now the Coventry District, were in the midst of seventeen members, and they were preparing to hold the first immersion in the church in America. There was no ordained minister this side of the Atlantic.
>
> The members hold a council. Peter Becker is chosen to act as elder. The preliminary examination is held, prayer is offered, and then these twenty-three souls walk out into

the winter afternoon, in single file, headed by Peter Becker. They journey to the Wissahickon Creek. The group kneels. Overhead the solemn sentinels of the forest fastness—the pines and hemlock—are stilled. The icebound stream utters strangely solemn music. . . . Peter Becker's voice breaks the stillness. The prayer is ended. The six candidates for membership in God's family are led one by one into the water and are baptized by trine immersion. The procession returns to Germantown.

They assembled in the house of John Gomorry (Gomre). It is evening now. The old-time tallow-dips are lighted. They gather about a long table, a hymn is sung, and in the silent evening hour, with no witness but God, and curious children, these people begin the observance of the ordinances of God's house on Christmas evening, 1723. The sisters on one side, the brethren on the other, arise and wash one another's feet. Then they eat the Lord's Supper, pass the kiss of charity with the right hand of fellowship, partake of the holy communion, sing a hymn, and go out.

At once we observe certain characteristics of early Brethren worship. The place of meeting is in a member's home. Lay leadership is evident. A running stream offers the setting for baptism—even in winter. The whole community of like-minded believers is involved. Hymns of praise are sung. Prayers are offered. The ceremonies they observe are simple, natural, as close to New Testament patterns as they can determine on the basis of their study and searching of the scriptures.

Two influential movements

In order to understand traditional Brethren attitudes toward worship as well as specific Brethren worship practices, we must recognize how much Brethren beginnings were influenced by two religious movements: pietism and anabaptism.

Pietism was a reform movement within German protestantism that emphasized meeting in small groups for Bible study and worship as a means of reforming the church. Pietists sought the practical application of religious beliefs in good works. They encouraged the building of hospitals and the sending of missionaries. They protested against the formalism and coldness of much public worship and rejected the dogmatism of the official church. The earliest Brethren were probably influenced by radical pietists who advocated separating from the state churches, turning against existing church structures, and trying to recover the "primitive Christianity" of the early Christian church.

Yet these first Brethren, unlike some of the other radical separatist groups, felt the need to be a church. Like the anabaptists with whom they were also in touch, they viewed the church as a fellowship of believers bound together as obedient disciples of Jesus Christ. He was example as well as Lord. Coming together in their homes for prayer and Bible study, they accepted the need for a church order and for observances that would be firmly grounded in the teachings of the New Testament and in the practice of the earliest Christians.

Given the background out of which the Brethren movement came, it is not surprising that their understanding of public worship would reject many traditional practices and emphasize others that were unknown or perhaps neglected in the more institutional churches. For example, Brethren, like other Pietist groups, met in private homes, partly because they could no longer worship in existing churches but also because they wanted to search the scriptures on their own and to seek the guidance of the Holy Spirit as they decided for themselves just what discipleship, or a literal following of the words and example of Jesus, would entail. In place of the usual sacraments they agreed to observe certain *ordinances* that were specifically outlined by the New Testament.

In seeking to become a New Testament church, our Brethren forerunners looked not only to the teachings of Jesus and the letters of Paul for their understanding of faith and for guidance as to how they should live; they turned just as eagerly to the scriptures to discover what acts of obedience, what specific worship forms, were expected of Christians. The result of their study, both of the New Testament and of early church history, was to become convinced of the need for certain practices or rites that they called ordinances. They chose this word rather than "sacrament," which means a ceremony regarded as holy or sacred, or something that is consecrated for religious use, sometimes considered also to dispense grace to the believer.

Brethren were more interested in being obedient to New Testament than in preserving churchly traditions. Because these ordinances, as Brethren understood and practiced them, often differed from the requirements of other churches, they were from the beginning a matter of controversy. Brethren writings were addressed to the defense of these marks of "primitive Christianity," and it is from such discussions that we learn not only what Brethren believed but also how they worshiped.

In place of highly liturgical services of worship following elaborate rituals and a calendar for the church year, they preferred informal services in which subjective personal experiences could be shared along with their Bible study and the singing of devotional hymns. In place of depending entirely upon ordained clergymen to conduct worship services, they regarded all members as equally called to participate and lead. In place of such aids to worship as churchly architecture and instrumental music (some early Brethren spoke sarcastically about the use of "fiddles, bass fiddles, whistles, organs, harps, oboes, French horns, and bagpipes" in other church services), they emphasized congregational singing.

The love feast—common and commemorative
The traditional Brethren love feast, as it has been observed with some variations but also with a surprising degree of continuity all through the church's history, offers the best example of Brethren worship convictions in practice. Brethren have tended to discount the importance of ritual, perhaps in oppostion to formal ceremonies they regard as lifeless. Yet their love feast and communion service provides a splendid exhibition of the way a ritual can enable worshipers to recall and reenact

the experience of the Upper Room and thereby to perpetuate the simple ceremonies that Jesus himself commended to his followers to be observed "in remembrance of me." Seeking to be as faithful as possible to the New Testament records, Brethren have encouraged their members to become participants in a continuing drama, one that not only looks back to the supper that Jesus shared with his friends, but which celebrates the present experience of fellowship and communion in the body of Christ, and even looks forward to the fulfillment of the kingdom of God.

Historically the Brethren love feast was regarded as the chief event in the life of a congregation. It was preceded by a visit of the deacons to the home of every member. The time was announced early so that friends from other congregations could attend. In many cases it required all day Saturday and most of Sunday. It began with a preaching service on Saturday in preparation for a lengthy love feast on Saturday evening, and concluded with services and a dinner on Sunday. It was a social occasion as well as a worship experience. The host church not only provided meals and lodging (utilizing the kitchen and upper story of a meetinghouse) for participants but even offered hospitality to curious onlookers.

The first act in the drama follows the narrative in John 13 in which Jesus not only washed the feet of his disciples but urged them to follow his example. In Brethren practice, individual members kneel down to wash the feet of a brother or sister and receive the same service from another. The ceremony is so common, (crude, in the opinion of some persons), so much like everyday exercises in washing and being washed, that its ritualistic and symbolic value may be overlooked. The basin and towel actually represent the kind of service that many regard as menial, the work of servants or slaves, or the duties expected of a house servant or a laborer. This, of course, is exactly the point of Jesus' example; and it may explain why, in the face of so understandable a teaching on his part, Christians seem reluctant to imitate their servant Lord. Yet the feetwashing ritual also, as Jesus made quite clear, under-scores our need for cleansing, a repeated need despite the forgiveness and mercy of God.

The Brethren tradition, therefore, takes the most common of symbols and uses them in a dramatic but simple way to affirm the values of cleansing and service. It calls for specific actions—you don't simply *talk* about service in the feetwashing ritual, you literally, bodily kneel to do it. And it also suggests what those values mean in daily life. Accompanied traditionally by hymn-singing, this act of the total love feast drama can create a mood by which the Upper Room and its picture of dis-cipleship can help to transform the most mundane relationships.

Brethren have always included, as the second act in their sequence of the total love feast, a family meal around tables, similar to the agape meals once con-sidered so important in the early Christian church. Often this portion of the service is spoken of as "the Lord's Supper"—in contrast to many other groups that use that expression for the eucharist or communion. Its underly-ing emphasis is on the commonality of believers who, in the act of eating a meal, bind themselves together more intimately as members of the family of God.

Brethren have insisted that while the meal they share resembles the Jewish passover—and that resemblance has at times helped to determine the menu—it is rather the table of Jesus that they recall. Paul, in one of the passages Brethren take as their authorization (1 Cor. 11:20-21) reminded the Corinthians that to eat the Lord's supper means being sensitive to the needs of all the members of the body. The emphasis is on the deepest dimensions of caring for one another; there must be more than a casual coming together, for the meal is an expression of *agape* love. Often in Brethren practice the meal has been a solemn one, eaten in silence. On other occasions it has taken on a more festive character since the spirit of joy and thanksgiving seems appropriate for this rich celebration. In either situation, persons seated around the table are not inclined to forget that it is the Lord's table.

The final act in the drama of the Upper Room that Brethren reenact is the communion service they share with Christians from many traditions. The breaking of the bread that symbolizes the body of Christ and the drinking from the cup that symbolizes his blood become the climax of the entire service. In one sense the earlier rituals prepare for it, but the deepest understanding of service, togetherness, and unity in Christ comes with our standing in wonder before his cross. For Brethren the elements are symbols that recall his crucifixion and death as well as the words that preceded them. These emblems, not sacred or magical in themselves, are memorials that work in a powerful way to draw attention to his sacrificial love, his giving of his life in order that we might live. In the communion service the real presence of Christ is understood as his presence in the body, the church.

Many years ago a prayer used in connection with the sharing of the bread and cup called upon God to bless them "from their common to the commemorative use." The total love feast and communion service, as Brethren have traditionally observed it, utilizes the most common objects: a basin, towel, table, ordinary food, water, bread, and grape juice, often in the most common surroundings. They are seen also as sacred because they recall the common things that Jesus himself employed, and thus they are commemorative. The Brethren love feast, perhaps because it does not utilize unusual elements, can help participants realize how significant are *all* the ordinary things of their everyday existence. So one purpose of feetwashing is to dignify every act of service and cleansing. One value of the Lord's Supper is to hallow every family meal. And some of the richest meanings of communion are realized when a Christian's whole life-style becomes a witness to sacrificial living.

Baptism and other ordinances
In recent years Brethren have tended to minimize or

perhaps simply to overlook the importance of baptism as an integral part of the church's corporate worship. The service itself, though it follows the traditional form of the ordinance that Brethren teach and observe, is frequently scheduled so that it invites the presence of family and friends but seldom involves the total congregation in a significant way. While it continues to be meaningful, if properly interpreted, for the new member and that person's close associates, it is seldom seen as an opportunity for the whole church to share in the joy of accepting another member into the body of Christ and thereby affirming and celebrating what membership means.

Consider some of the rich worship values that the Brethren form of baptism by threefold immersion offers. It requires not only a verbal confession of faith, expressed openly in an examination period, but it asks also for participating in a physical act that involves the total person, the act of complete immersion in water. The Brethren mode of baptism symbolically pictures the need for cleansing from sin. It follows instructions clearly set forth in the New Testament that recognize God as Father, Son, and Spirit. (Matt. 28:19; Acts 2:38; 8:36-38; Rom. 6:3-5). It calls for identification in a symbolic way with the death and resurrection of Jesus. And it encourages the newly baptized member to walk in newness of life.

The particular form of baptism Brethren observe, though well grounded in biblical authority and sanctioned by early Christian practice, has often been the subject of controversy and debate—often with other religious groups. The need now is not for such argumentation, but rather for a rediscovery of the congregation's part in the initiation rites it requires. It should not be necessary to require immersion out of doors in running water with the congregation singing hymns by the riverside to recapture the worship values associated with baptism. In our churches, equipped as most of them are with baptistries, we should still be able to plan services that dramatize the individual's part in trine immersion while inviting the whole congregation to demonstrate just as openly its acceptance and support of each new member.

In his pamphlet on "The Meaning of Baptism," William Beahm notes that a "Christian conviction underlying baptism is the reality and relevance of the church. Not only is baptism a means of individual salvation; it is also an initiatory ceremony by which we become members of the church, the body of Christ and fellowship of the Holy Spirit. 'For in one spirit were we all baptized into one body' (1 Cor. 12:13)."

The anointing service is often regarded as a private matter for someone seriously ill, primarily for family members and close friends. But the service can be and has been—in some localities—a public service of healing of benefit to many worshipers. It involves an invitation from a person, not necessarily critically ill, who wishes to be anointed. The familiar scripture from James 5:14-16 is read. There is an opportunity for the confession of sin and a statement of personal faith. Prayers are essential; sometimes there is a hymn. The ceremony of anointing with oil is a simple but meaningful ritual that strengthens faith and frequently restores physical health.

Brethren also practice the laying on of hands for times of ordination or commissioning for special ministries. The congregation is involved regularly in such services. At similar occasions at Annual Conference the entire denomination is at least represented in the service.

Following New Testament instructions, Brethren used to "greet each other with a holy kiss." Sometimes a warm handshake or an embrace is substituted. The ritual is similar to the practice of some other Christian groups who "pass the peace" from hand to hand with spoken blessings for each worshiper.

Convictions regarding worship

Lest we make too much of what Brethren have rejected in the services of other groups, consider the positive worship values they derived trom their insistence that their church should be patterned on the New Testament. Among many characteristics emphasized by Brethren, the following can be noted:

1. *Worship encompasses all of life* (James 1:22-27; Matt. 5:23-24). Worship can never be considered only in the context of a Sunday service or a ceremonial observance. The New Testament repeatedly contends that the way we live every moment of every day is part of our worship; that our thoughts and actions on weekdays may be more indicative of our effectiveness in worship than our Sunday ceremonies. Just as faith without works is dead, so is worship without daily commitment to God and neighbor. The epistle of James insists that we must act upon the word we hear in worship, and Jesus made it clear that we cannot make an appropriate offering to God if we are seriously at odds with our brothers and sisters.

2. *Worship issues in service, and service is a means of worship* (2 Cor. 9:11-14). One of the words most commonly applied to public worship is the word "liturgy." It is frequently understood to refer to specific orders of worship associated with Sunday services, or, in some traditions, with the eucharist or communion service. But the New Testament use of the same words implies a broader meaning. Liturgy is literally the work or the service of the people. It can mean service to the world through the church just as properly as it can mean what we call "divine worship." Observe how Paul, in writing to the Corinthians about the splendid sharing on the part of the Macedonian churches, insists that such generosity will produce thanksgiving, and that such service to the needy "overflows in thanksgiving to God." He claims that they "glorify God"—surely an act of worship—by their generosity.

3. *Worship requires integrity* (Matt. 6:1-18). There is no place in worship for hypocrisy or pretense or insincerity. Jesus was unsparing in his condemnation of those who paraded their piety in their public prayers, in their almsgiving, or in their fasting. He called for integrity in worship as opposed to ceremonies in public places that depended on empty phrases, many words, and the hollow display of religious intentions. Instead he counseled modesty, even secrecy, in the way one worships.

And he offered a model prayer to illustrate the basic elements of true worship. Brethren were impressed with those words—even to the point of making the Lord's Prayer almost mandatory for a worship service.

4. *Worship involves a fellowship of believers* (Acts 2:43-47; 1 Cor. 12:12-14, 27). Though the New Testament encourages individual prayer and private devotion, its writers place major emphasis on worship as a communal activity, in which an entire congregation participates. The group that experiences the presence of Christ among them may be small ("two or three gathered together in my name") or it may encompass a multitude as on the day of Pentecost, but in each case the worshipers themselves in their fellowship, in their togetherness, are identified with the very body of Christ. Such a "life together" has been a part of the Brethren experience, observed not only in the small group of eight whose baptism marked the beginning of the church but in a continuing emphasis on face-to-face relationships.

5. *Worship is every member's responsibility* (Gal. 6:1-5; Eph. 5:15-20; James 5:13-16; 1 Peter 2:4-10). For Brethren the "priesthood of all believers" affirmed by the Protestant Reformation meant not only that there was no need for a priestly mediator to stand between the believer and God, or for a specially consecrated person to fulfill ceremonial functions in worship; the concept also carried with it a sense of personal responsibility for each believer to be a priest to others. The instructions from the Epistle of James that described the anointing service said, "Confess your sins to one another" as well as "pray for one another." And Paul, in writing to the Galatians said, "If anyone is overtaken in any trespass, you who are spiritual should restore that person in a spirit of gentleness." So also in worship each participant shares in the responsibility for singing hymns, praying, and sharing personal testimonies. A description of the Brethren in the year 1770 indicates that "every brother is allowed to speak in a way of exhortation and expounding." Today we would take care to include sisters in the invitation.

6
Brethren at Worship: Some Values Remain

With what shall I come before the Lord,
and bow myself before God on high? . . .
What does the Lord require of you
but to do justice, and to love kindness,
and to walk humbly with your God?
Micah 6:6a, 8

The place of worship seems modest, as churches go. You enter the door, shake the welcoming hand of a greeter, listen to quiet music from an electronic organ, follow an usher to a place near a window whose colored glass diffuses light across a gathering congregation. The pews seem solid but comfortable; and you glance at the bulletin you were given, noting an order of service that should not be too difficult to follow.

You have come to participate in a fairly typical Sunday worship service in the 1970's in the Church of the Brethren. The choir enters, followed by the pastor, who takes his/her place behind a lectern. You join in the call to worship, a scriptural invitation mimeographed on your bulletin. The choir leads as you stand to sing the Gloria Patri and remain standing for an invocation prayer and a hymn of praise.

There is a slight change of mood, a kind of loosening away from seriousness, when you learn that now is the "sharing time," a period to introduce visitors, to overflow with some happy news, or to look for some other shoulders to help carry your burdens. There may be laughter or tears. You may be urged to pray about and support some cause. Or you may be instructed to turn around and greet your neighbors.

The pastor guides you into more serious moments as you take your part in a responsive or unison reading, listen to an anthem by the choir, contribute your gift to the offering, and stand to sing the Doxology. And you sing again, this time a hymn concerned less about God's majesty and more about your personal experience of faith or trust.

Without your observing just when or where, the pastor has gone to the pulpit, well-equipped for amplification and projection of the message. The chancel before you is open, so that you have an unobstructed view of the focal center, perhaps an altar, more likely a table, where flowers and visual symbols catch your eye.

Following the sermon you stand to sing a hymn of dedication, remain for the benediction (not always offered with hands raised in a parting blessing), and for a choral response. The organ postlude is louder that the prelude. You are free to begin at once the visiting that is an evident sign of a relationship in which members find support and strangers know they are welcome.

The way it was before
Now, in your imagination, turn back the pages of time for more than a hundred years, and observe another Brethren service, also described as being fairly typical of its period. Your host is Henry R. Holsinger, a minister, editor, and historian, who wanted future generations to catch something of the spirit and flavor of the meetinghouse service he remembered. The time is "about the middle of the nineteenth century." He begins:

Let us now take a look at the old meetinghouse and its surroundings. It usually stands in some stately grove of old oaks, but is not itself a stately or imposing edifice. It is generally a long, low building, capable of seating a large congregation. . . . Neither inside nor outside was a dollar spent for any sort of ornamentation. The style of architecture was bare in its simplicity, and far removed from such vanities as spires, towers, stained windows, painted or cushioned pews, ornamental pulpits, or anything else which could not show the passport of indispensable utility.

Let us stand among the grand old oaks, and witness the gathering of the faithful. . . . The members, having alighted from their plain, almost rude vehicles, are greeting one another with the holy kiss. They linger around the church doors in quiet converse. . . .

Our description concerns a typical Tunker congregation, such as could be seen anywhere in the fraternity about the middle of the nineteenth century. Meeting day, which was usually only once a month at the old church, was the great Sabbath of the month. All who were physically able to be out, were sure to be there. . . .

They loved one another, and they loved to meet and greet each other at the doors of the sanctuary. They loved the plain gospel hymns, full of consolation and rest. They loved the glorious congregational singing, which swelled triumphantly in the great church, and rolled its billows of sublime harmony out through windows and doors, and up through the solemn oaks toward heaven. . . .

The congregation is in its place. Behind the long, unpainted table, instead of a pulpit, the long, plain bench is filled with the elders and preachers. There are no upholstered chairs for this unpretentious clergy. They allow themselves no luxury denied to the people.

A steady, strong, musical voice on the deacons' bench raises the tune, and soon the whole congregation join in the hearty singing. This was always the most attractive part of the old-time Tunker service. No congregation every sang better. It was a beautiful, spiritual, refreshing worship, and the sound of an instrument in one of those old-time Tunker congregations, where every voice made "melody unto the Lord," would have seemed a discord and a profanation.

But the hymn, lined out in a rather unnatural and sanctimonious style, is finished. Every verse was sung. The Sabbath is before them. No conventional hour shall limit the heavenly feast. The echoes of the last notes having died away, the preacher prepares to further enforce the sentiment of the hymn, and gradually prepare the minds of the people for prayer. His remarks are a prosy repetition of the sentiment of the lines, but they do not seem to be superfluous, or out of place. There must be no hurry on the threshold of the mercy-seat. . . .

The preacher calls to prayer. Immediately a great rustling is heard throughout the church. Every man and woman is on bended knees. No resting of foreheads on hands or bench backs will suffice to express the reverent spirit of the congregation. The leader in prayer tarries long at the mercy-seat. He may not be gifted, though many of the old brethren were gifted in this grace. They spake not the eloquence of the schools, but the eloquence of the heart, which, after all, is the truest eloquence. The seeming formality of the prayer is lightened by the evident sincerity of the man. Some prayed aloud the same prayer for years, without becoming wearisome or disappointing. Like a chapter in the Bible, it never grows old.

The initial season of devotion having closed, the oldest bishop extends "the liberty" to his associates, who, in turn, offer it to each other. This interchange of courtesies occupies a minute or more, the congregation meanwhile looking on, and wondering who would deliver the sermon, a point that in few congregations was settled before the time had actually arrived. If there happens to be a visiting brother on the bench, he usually finds it impossible to decline the "liberty." If there are none, one of the home ministers yields, with apparent reluctance, to the importunities of the brethren, and arises to sound forth the Word.

Lifting the big Bible from the stand, the preacher of the day, while looking for his text, or perhaps while trying to decide what text he would take, requests the congregation to sing either one or the other of two well-known hymns: "Father, I stretch my hands to Thee," or "A charge to keep I have." . . .

Deep feeling, not the kind which takes emotional forms, for the Tunkers are not and never were an emotional people, but the kind which springs from profound sincerity, inward truth, marks the singing of this hymn, and the preacher arises to his task.

The sermon finally concluded, a word of testimony is borne by one of the associate preachers, and this is

followed by the concluding prayer and hymn. Then, with
the usual announcements, the congregation is dis-
missed without the benediction, to return to the beautiful farms and fragrant orchards, the better benediction
of God's peace resting upon each one he carries with
him the consciousness of duty done, the sanctified memories of a holy place, and the sweet echoes of melody
and song.

Some things have changed

Even if the church we visit today should happen to be
located in the wooded grove where once a meetinghouse
stood, the changes that have come with more than a century are obvious to our eyes—and to our ears. Brethren
worship patterns have shifted, perhaps undergoing as
many remodelings and replacements as our places of
worship. It may help us to know how best to appropriate
our heritage if we note some of the developments, not
always improvements, in the setting and the manner of
our public services.

1. *From meetinghouse to sanctuary.* Built of stone,
brick or wood, the meetinghouse of earlier years was of
rectangular shape, with two doors, one for men and one
for women, on the long side. Sometimes the benches on
the narrow ends faced the center, but almost always a
table on the same level with the benches provided a place
from which local ministers could speak. There was no
pulpit or lectern or altar. The environment for worship
was extremely simple, with perhaps only a row of black
bonnets on one wall to match a row of black, broadbrim
hats on another.

From such emphasis on plainness, Brethren moved
toward adopting many characteristics of other Protestant
churches as they built in urban areas and even when it
was necessary to remodel or replace an earlier building.
Buildings were still rectangular, but one narrow side offered a single entrance and the other end provided a
raised area either for a central pulpit and a choir or for a
divided chancel with a communion table or altar at the
center. Decoration was gradually accepted with colored
glass, flowers in season, occasional paintings. More

recently some churches have chosen ecclesiastical furniture and furnishings that employ symbols and designs associated with liturgical tradition. Even though some Brethren today are reluctant to call their meetingplace a "church" or "sanctuary," hardly anyone regards it as a meetinghouse.

2. *From farmer preachers to professional ministers.* The congregation of one hundred years ago was unlikely to have any paid or professionally trained minister, but there was a certain order in its leadership. Though the ministers and elders sat on the same level with their brothers and sisters just as they worked through the week at similar tasks to support themselves, there was a presiding elder with authority to lead and to "extend the liberty" of speaking to other ministers. A deacon might also assist in reading the Bible, lining a hymn, leading in prayer, or giving a testimony. In such ways leadership was shared, though rarely were women invited to contribute to public worship.

The move from rural to urban and suburban churches, the encouragement of a multiplicity of programs for all age groups, the development of community-centered services and ministries, and the emphasis on special training for ministers—all of these and many other factors have caused congregations to employ pastors, associate pastors, choir leaders, and organists, who assume many of the leadership roles in worship today. But many so trained would be the first to emphasize that their function is not to replace lay members or to diminish their participation in worship; rather, they see themselves as enablers, using their skills to free many more members for fuller involvement in mission—and worship.

3. *From a capella to accompanied singing.* Imagine a church without a piano or organ. Most Brethren congregations, however, seemed to do quite well, until the present century, without any kind of instrumental music. While, as we shall note later, they produced hymnbooks in surprising quantities, they could raise their songs of praise without the aid of German or English texts,

without reading regular or shaped notes. The solution was in "lining" hymns, a practice that has been followed at various times in the history of group singing. A deacon would choose a tune in the meter of the words of a familiar hymn. Then he would speak or sing the first line or two of the hymn, to be followed by the congregation. He would repeat with additional lines, and the response would follow.

Singing schools and music classes aided the development of church music, and eventually churches accepted the piano or organ as a support to their hymn singing and as a means of creating an atmosphere for worship. Most Brethren churches value congregational singing today. While they enjoy the contribution of instruments and even of electronic reproductions of music, they are not inclined to turn the music of praise totally over to professional musicians.

4. *From a simple outline to a printed program.* Reading the accounts of earlier Brethren services—in the 1700's and the 1800's—we must observe that they were neither so spontaneous or so unprogramed as we might have thought. Anything associated with the ordinances was expected to follow a New Testament order. And custom, if not the scriptures, often dictated how worship rituals were followed. Yet the feeling was informal, and in most cases there were opportunities for personal testimonies or brief exhortations.

But in the late nineteenth century a move toward more regularity in basic ceremonies could be observed. A *Brethren's Church Manual* was published in 1887, to be followed by many other manuals for ministers and books describing order and polity. One of the most recent, *Book of Worship, Church of the Brethren,* provides suggested outlines and resources for "the service of corporate worship," resources for the Christian year, guidance for observing rites and ordinances, and suggested patterns for a variety of occasional services.

5. *From extended family to a search for community.* Some of the changes we have noted may be misunderstood unless we perceive how, in the same period of

time, the complexion of the congregation has changed. Many rural congregations were composed, a century ago, of several interrelated families who lived as neighbors in a well-defined community. Their nonconformity with the world was marked by visible signs that helped them identify themselves as Brethren. The family reunion quality of their assemblies was one ingredient of their worship.

Today the Brethren who gather for worship are usually separated from such roots, if they ever had them. They may even have little in common with next-door neighbors. But their needs as persons to be a part of a supporting community are just as great; even greater is their need for identification in visible ways with the body of Christ. For some, a district conference or an Annual Conference offers worship experiences reminiscent of "family reunion" memories. But for most persons, congregational worship and fellowship provide the only means to discover their togetherness in the body of Christ.

Some values remain
Despite the conditions that make for change, some worship values that Brethren have cherished through the years still remain. They are worth noting, worth exploring and perhaps even exploiting a little, since they contribute to Brethren identity even as they have something to offer in ecumenical experiences.

1. *Hymn making and hymn singing.* While Brethren were still in Europe, only a few short years after their coming together as a distinctive church, they produced in 1720 their first hymnal. Along with hymns from current German hymnals that appealed to the "Baptist-minded," they included a hundred new hymns, "most of which were written by brethren who have been imprisoned . . . for the sake of their witness to Jesus." The book, which contains also a hymn by Alexander Mack, Sr., "Count Well the Cost," (Number 36, *The Brethren Songbook*) was introduced with the prayer that God would "grant all blessing and grace here in this world-wilderness to serve God in spite of this in spirit and in truth, and also

to sing hymns to the Lord in spirit."

The same conviction encouraged Christopher Sauer, Sr. to publish a hymnal in 1744 under the title *Das Kleine Davidische Psalterspiel* (The Little Davidic Psalter) which involved making a careful selection of around 500 hymns from an earlier German collection (of more than 1,000 lengthy hymns) widely used by pietist, separatist, and Mennonite groups in Europe. Many of the tunes in the collection are identical with chorales harmonized by Bach. German-speaking colonists sang from this hymnbook as three more editions (1760, 1767, and 1777) were published by Christopher Sauer, Jr. At least fourteen editions were eventually published in German. Among the hymns were original contributions by Alexander Mack, Sr., Alexander Mack, Jr., Peter Becker, and John Naas, all Brethren leaders.

The first Brethren hymnal in English was *The Christian's Duty,* printed by Peter Leibert in 1791. Other editions followed. The collection introduced a number of standard English hymns, including nineteen that have appeared also in every Brethren hymnal since that time. It was likely used chiefly by Brethren who spoke English during the first half of the nineteenth century.

In 1852 Henry Kurtz published *A Choice Selection of Hymns* in English. In 1868 he compiled a new collection of German hymns. At the instruction of Annual Conference, James Quinter in 1867 published *The Brethren's Hymn Book,* a selection of 818 hymns. For the first time the authors' of hymns were identified. The next two Brethren hynmnals (1872 and 1879) used the same texts but added tunes. Later hymnals, also authorized by Annual Conference, appeared in 1901, 1926, and 1951. As a supplement to *The Brethren Hymnal* (1951), new hymns and songs are now added periodically to a loose-leaf collection called *The Brethren Songbook.* The current hymnal contains 53 texts or tunes that have been provided by Brethren authors and composers. It includes translations of hymns by such early Brethren leaders as Alexander Mack, Sr., Alexander Mack, Jr., John Naas, and Christopher Sauer, Jr.

This brief recital of hymn publishing can barely do more than suggest how central to Brethren worship has been the congregational singing of hymns. Such singing, especially at conferences, assemblies, and camps, as well as in many churches, still represents a distinctive quality in our worship.

2. *Respect for the Word.* More than many Brethren worshipers may be aware, the materials we use and the customs we follow—today as in the earliest meetings—reflect a heritage of respect for the Word of God. Not only the obvious scripture readings, but the texts of hymns and anthems, the spirit and phrasing of prayers, and especially the traditional ceremonial ordinances, derive their shape and form from biblical patterns. Sermons today may be more topical and less textual than in centuries past, but even today worshipers often express to speakers their hunger for the eternal Word and their eagerness to learn what God's Spirit is saying to them and to the church.

3. *Lay participation.* In a former chapter we noted the Brethren conviction that worship is every member's responsibility. With the employment of a professionally trained ministry, some congregations were undoubtedly tempted to relegate much of that responsibility for worship direction to the pastor or to professional musicians. And some ministers may have claimed such leadership as their right. But increasingly the gifts—talents, skills, crafts, abilities, as well as what might be regarded as more specific spiritual gifts—of lay members are now being welcomed for the enrichment of all kinds of services. There are hardly any bars to lay leadership in any function today. There are hopeful signs that the original Brethren concept of the church as the people of God, equally responsible before God and each other for service and praise, will come into its own in ways that can bring new life in today's church.

4. *Celebration of the community.* Some ceremonies that used to be a little austere and removed from the worshipers in the pew have been opened recently to include the whole community of faith. The "sharing time"

of today's services relates the experiences of members more closely to the church, and on many occasions (welcoming new members, dedicating babies, installing new leaders) worshipers are invited to come forward to form a "circle of love" around those who receive special recognition. In other churches there appears to be a new freedom to share spiritual experiences in times of testimony and witness. And some of the deeper levels of caring—at times of pain and sorrow, at moments of confession when words of assurance are exchanged—are now at last being consciously recognized in simple ceremonies when members affirm one another, make their mutual support visible, and pray for and with each other. The church seems recently to have discovered what it once knew but almost forgot—that people are more important than organs and choirs, steeples or altars, ceremonies or customs.

5. *Openness to new understanding.* From the beginning, Brethren were unwilling to let their insights and interpretations, though they would argue for them vigorously, become hardened into a creed that would be binding or a liturgy that would be limiting. At times, in holding fast to the truths they affirmed, it must have been easy to overlook this modest approach to finality, this reminder that God is still active and that, even through the pages of the New Testament, the Spirit will have new truths to impart.

Today the same openness to new understanding— and to new patterns, new styles, new ways of worship— can help congregations deal with diversity within each congregation and with a wide range of worship tastes such as those represented now at any Annual Conference. With such a traditional concern for "being open" Brethren should be able to sing many a new song to the Lord and to find for themselves what Paul desired for the troubled Corinthian church—the acceptance of "varieties of gifts," "varieties of service," "varieties of working," but always the same Spirit.

7
Making the Most of Time: Days and Seasons of the Christian Year

This is the day which the Lord has made;
Let us rejoice and be glad in it. Ps. 118:24 (RSV)

Any day will do, but New Year's Day may be the best time for your entire family to decorate the calendar. Try putting circles around the birthdays of family and friends. Underline important anniversaries. Block out vacation periods from school and from work. Put a warning flag beside the days when bills come due or obligations must be faced. Note the times when seasons change, when the house or farm must be readied and clothing mended to prepare for summer or winter. Do you make an annual pilgrimage to somewhere back East, down South, up North or out West? Mark it well. Do you honor Lincoln and Washington, or Martin Luther King, Jr. on their birthdays? In one way or another the calendar serves you, but if you don't watch out it can also be your master. Time is a gift, made available in the same generous measure, to everyone, but care must be taken to make the most of it.

Guidelines for setting special occasions for worship

Christians have differed in the emphasis they give to times and seasons. Before you examine the observances that make up your own "Christian year," consider these words of counsel from the scriptures:

"Making the most of time." The phrase comes from the Epistle to the Ephesians, where another translation puts it "redeeming the time, because the days are evil." The writer is talking about distinctive marks of the Christian life-style, wanting the Ephesian Christians to take advantage of every opportunity for good in a time when many things are evil. In this same context the writer advocates worship expressions involving singing and giving thanks (Eph. 5:15-20).

"Teach us to number our days." What the psalmist asks for is far more than turning the leaves in our datebooks or planning ahead for another year. It is rather to live our allotted days and years in the awareness that "from everlasting to everlasting thou art God." Because of God's steadfast love "we may rejoice and be glad all our days," and that prospect includes the calendar but also goes far beyond it (Psalm 90:1-4, 9-12, 14-15).

"For everything there is a season." Although every day and every hour is important, there are times more appropriate for some activities than for others. The list of times and seasons you adopt for personal use or the outline that you follow in group worship may be quite different from the comprehensive listing offered by the writer of Ecclesiastes. But the wisdom of his observations has good counsel for us, at least in reminding us that "for everything there is a season" (Eccles. 3:1-8).

"One day as better than another." In making the most of time, some persons give a heavy priority to certain days, and indeed they are important. But Paul recognized the validity of differences when it came to scruples about eating or abstaining, about observing or not observing certain days. So his advice is to consider the convictions of others about observances, not rushing into judgment, but rather being careful not to

cause a brother or sister to stumble. If you observe special days, says Paul, do so in honor of the Lord. If you consider all days equal in holiness, do this also in honor of the Lord. Paul's counsel provides an excellent guideline for our consideration of the diverse ways in which Christians regard the calendar (Romans 14:5-10).

"The Sabbath was made for man, not man for the Sabbath." An issue that frequently set Jesus over against the Pharisees concerned the proper observance of the Sabbath. He insisted that this special day was holy not simply in terms of its prohibitions, but rather for its opportunities "to do good" and "to save life." Whatever we decide about the days or seasons we set apart for celebration and special attention, we need to see them not as binding but as liberating us to act as Christians (Mark 2:23 — 3:4).

The Jewish ceremonial year

Sabbath rules and Sabbath customs have played a significant part in Jewish worship. The importance of a day of rest was noted in the story of creation and confirmed by one of the Ten commandments. While it was marked by certain taboos against working, it was also a time for joy and worship, for rest and instruction. But certain days and seasons in the year are also important in Jewish observance. These begin in the fall with high holy days including the new year *Rosh Hashana* and *Yom Kippur,* the day of atonement. Soon thereafter is the feast of booths, called *Succoth,* at late harvest, a time of thanksgiving. Near our Christmas, Jews observe *Chanukah,* the feast of lights. The feast of lots, or *Purim,* is a time of banqueting and joy. *Passover,* the feast of unleavened bread, is familiar to Christians because of the part it played in the final days of Jesus' ministry. *Pentecost,* or the feast of weeks, celebrates the first harvest and the giving of the Ten Commandments. Christians observe the same time, but call attention rather to the early church's experience with the Holy Spirit. Though our own ceremonies are different, Christians need to be aware of Jewish observances.

The development of a Christian Year

In the early years of the Christian church, worship celebrations centered around the Sunday gatherings in which the Lord's Supper, including an agape meal, was regularly observed. Easter time was the chief season for rejoicing. But as the church grew in numbers, especially after it became officially recognized and was supported by the state, the observances of special days rapidly multiplied. By the end of the fourth century the Christian Year had developed a basic outline which is still widely observed.

This ceremonial year, which seeks to recall events in the life of Christ and the implications of his gospel, is divided into two parts. The first, which begins with Advent and continues through Ascension Day, is often called the Lord's half-year (God speaking to human beings through revelation). The second part is regarded as the church's half-year (the believers' response to God) and is concerned with the teachings of Christ.

The Protestant Reformation sought to do away with many observances, particularly Saints days and some festivals not grounded in biblical events, while retaining the important events in the church's calendar. Then came separatist groups that rejected many customs and ceremonies, holding only to Sunday worship. The Quakers even insisted that Sunday be known simply as "the first day."

These more drastic reforms sought to purify the church and its worship. But along with casting out traditional observances that had been abused, they frequently allowed a vacuum to develop, so that many of the free churches, including the Church of the Brethren, while free of a liturgical calendar, easily accepted other annual observances into their schedules. What has occurred is that, for all practical purposes, many churches now have a calendar that is partly traditional and biblical, partly patriotic (as national holidays are included), partly promotional (as various good causes are recognized), and partly local (as congregations adapt to the communities they serve).

A strict following of the liturgical Christian year usually involves the use of a lectionary, a table of Bible readings for every Sunday in the year. Even those churches, like the Church of the Brethren, that follow the liturgical year only in part, often provide a recommended schedule of readings for the benefit of pastors and for the private use of individuals who want their reading of the scriptures to be more than casual. The most recent Book of Worship for the Church of the Brethren suggests readings from the psalms, the Old Testament, the gospels, and the epistles for a two-year cycle, as well as proposed readings for love feast and communion and for special days in the church year.

Some advantages of following a lectionary are that it insures attention to major portions of the Bible and consideration of basic doctrines. It provides a way, similar to that of Uniform Bible lessons, for Christians of various traditions around the world to unite in certain areas of worship and praise. Many church leaders feel the need for such an outline to assist them in their planning. Yet others, who cherish and exercise more freedom in the Spirit, prefer to allow more opportunity for spontaneous activity, even in their reading of the scriptures.

A calendar of days and seasons
(Following are brief descriptions of the special days, weeks, and seasons that are commonly considered in the functional calendar that many churches follow. Some reflect the historical and liturgical events observed for centuries. Others provide for the celebration of values important to Christians today. A few take into consideration the special concerns of Brethren worshipers.)

Epiphany. January 6, The word "epiphany" means manifestation. In western churches worshipers often recognize at this time the coming of wise men from the east to worship Jesus (Matt. 2:1-12). The day is sometimes called Three Kings Day. In worship services, usually on the Sunday preceding, the emphasis is on the meaning of Christ for the whole world. Eastern Orthodox churches choose January 6 as the time for their celebration of the birth of Jesus and also of his baptism.

Twelfth Night. January 6. In many parts of the world the season of Christmas begins on Christmas eve and continues for twelve days, ending in festivities on the "twelfth night."

Week of Prayer. January. Many Protestant churches designate the first full week in January as a week of prayer, often observed in ecumenical services. In recent years the World Council of Churches has encouraged the observance of the third week in January as a "Week of Prayer for Christian Unity."

Lent. The season of Lent is a forty-day period of personal devotion and discipline in preparation for Easter. The name comes from an Anglo-Saxon word for Spring. The period of time recalls the forty days Moses spent on Sinai and the forty days Jesus spent in the wilderness. Only weekdays are counted in the period. Many churches, including some that do not follow a liturgical calendar, plan special services and observances during Lent.

Shrove Tuesday. The day preceding the beginning of Lent takes its name from the custom of "shriving"—of confessing sins and receiving absolution. In some places it is celebrated as a final feast before fasting, associated with pancakes in England and with Mardi Gras (fat Tuesday) revelries in other countries.

Ash Wednesday. The first day of Lent is observed by Roman Catholic and by some Protestant churches as a day of penitence. In some ceremonies a priest will place ashes (from palm branches of the previous year) on the forehead of a worshiper.

World Day of Prayer. First Friday in Lent. Church women from around the globe sponsor a worldwide circle of prayer and Bible study.

One Great Hour of Sharing. Fourth Sunday in Lent. Though promoted as an offering emphasis in support of sharing with the hungry and homeless, observances on this day are characterized by worship themes related to sharing and service.

Passion Sunday. Fifth Sunday in Lent. A day when Roman Catholic churches—and some Protestant churches also—place emphasis on the suffering of Christ.

Holy Week. The week before Easter. Holy week observances developed within the church soon after the Christian faith received official recognition. It offered a means of recalling a series of historical events and teaching their significance to new converts.

Palm Sunday. The Sunday before Easter. This day is almost universally observed in commemoration of Jesus' triumphal entry into Jerusalem (John 12:12-16). As a festival it originated in the fourth century in Jerusalem, where pilgrims joined a procession from the Mount of Olives to the city.

Maundy Thursday. The Thursday before Easter. The word "maundy" is derived from a Latin word for "commandment" and refers to Jesus giving his disciples a new commandment that they love one another. For Brethren the evening is an especially appropriate time for the complete love feast and communion service (John 13:1-15). Other traditions observe the feetwashing in a limited manner when rulers or church leaders publicly wash the feet of a few persons.

Good Friday. The Friday before Easter. Many Protestant and some Roman Catholic churches conduct a three-hour service, from noon to 3 p.m., during which the seven words from the cross are read and pondered. Often Catholic churches provide opportunity for worshipers to "venerate" the cross and to follow the fourteen stations of the cross.

Easter. The date of Easter varies from year to year— and sometimes from church to church. Western churches celebrate the festival on the Sunday after the first full moon following the Spring equinox (between March 21 and April 25). The English word for Easter comes from the name of the Saxon goddess of dawn. Other languages use words derived from the Hebrew word for Passover. Most western churches celebrate the resurrection on Easter morning, sometimes at sunrise. Eastern Orthodox churches time their Saturday evening services so that at midnight, when an officiating priest announces that "Christ is risen," worshipers quickly light candles and respond that "Christ is risen indeed."

Family Week, or Festival of the Christian Home. First full week in May. In place of earlier observances of Mother's Day, Father's Day and Children's Day, many Protestant churches observe the second Sunday in May or the days just preceding it as a time to celebrate family relationships in a Christian context.

Rural Life Sunday. Fifth Sunday after Easter. Traditionally this was Rogation Sunday, a time when a procession around a parish would help to confirm its boundaries. It was also a time of intercession for crops. Protestant churches often call attention to rural life values and stewardship of the soil on this occasion.

Pentecost. Seven weeks after Easter. Also called Whitsunday, Pentecost is one of the oldest Christian celebrations, commemorating the gift of the Holy Spirit (Acts 2) on what some have called the birthday of the church. The word Pentecost signifies the number 50. The Jewish Pentecost was fifty days after the Passover. For many years it was customary for Brethren to schedule their Annual Meeting so that it came at Pentecost, thus signifying the desire of the church to be directed by the Holy Spirit.

Annual Conference. For the Church of the Brethren, Annual Conference is such a central and unifying experience that it affects the sequence of many events in the life of the church. In recent years, for practical reasons, the denomination's annual meeting has been held in early summer normally near the end of June.

World Communion Sunday. First Sunday in October. Since communion, in one form or another, is common to almost all churches, many Protestant churches schedule their fall observance for this time as an ecumenical witness.

Reformation Sunday. The Sunday nearest Oct. 31. Remembering the day in 1517 when Martin Luther nailed his famous theses to the Wittenberg chapel door, this observance recalls the Reformation.

Universal Bible Sunday. Formerly second Sunday in December. Now third Sunday in November. A day that calls special attention to Bible reading, Bible translation, and Bible distribution.

Thanksgiving Day. Fourth Thursday in November. Though determined by government proclamation and often limited to national thanksgiving, this American holiday is widely observed by congregational or community services of worship and praise. It bears some similarity to the harvest festivals of the Hebrews.

Advent. Sunday nearest November 30. Advent is the beginning of the traditional Christian year. The four Sundays that precede Christmas emphasize expectancy and preparation, awakening and anticipation. Advent candles, Advent wreaths, and Advent calendars utilize various symbols to mark the season.

Christmas Eve and Christmas December 24 and 25. For some Christians, the celebration of Christmas does not officially begin until Christmas eve, when many churches now have special candlelight services. Though Christmas itself is probably now the most beloved of Christian festivals, it was not observed until early in the third century. The day was set at the time of a pagan Roman festival.

8
Wonderful Words of Life: Language in Worship

And they read from the book, from the law of God, clearly; and they gave the sense, so that the people understood the reading. Neh. 8:8 (RSV)

You always feel a little anxious when you cross national borders. It's not only your concern whether your papers are in order; you also know that you may feel strange in a place where customs are different and the language is not your own.

Some persons think that entering a church and sharing in a worship service is like visiting a foreign country. The atmosphere itself may be in sharp contrast to what is outside, but mostly it's the language that creates the sense of strangeness. Not that many services are actually conducted in another language—you can hear a few Latin or Greek phrases, an occasional Hebrew word— the trouble seems to be with English. The readings may come from a translation of the Bible dating back 350 years. If there is a rather formal liturgy, its phrases differ from the common speech you use. And even the hymns seem to have a language of their own, singing to a God "which wert and art and evermore shalt be."

Of course, if you have been faithful in church atten-

ance and if your training in church school was thorough,
you can pray the Lord's Prayer beginning, "Our Father,
which art in heaven" or listen to readings about
"cherubim and seraphim" and not even smile when the
choir sings about "the Holy Ghost." But even so, you
may wonder why there are so many words that seem to
belong only in church. The way you speak almost
everywhere else doesn't fit the patterns of "religious"
speech.

If the purpose of worship is to provide an escape
from the everyday world, then a special language would
be exactly what you needed, a language filled with secret
code words and signs and symbols that only members
would understand. But we are eager for another kind of
worship—"in spirit and in truth," as Jesus said—which
relates to all of life, the kind of worship that provides an
opportunity for meeting, for us to come face to face with
God and with our brothers and sisters. So we have a
right to ask of language that it really aid our communication with God and with one another.

This does not mean that every word we speak must
be short and simple to everyone. Actually we are dealing
with insights and relationships that are continually
developing and changing. So we should expect, as we
grow in understanding, to find new words we can make
our own. And there are traditional expressions that are
rich in meaning and not too difficult to comprehend.
There is also the language of scripture that comes alive
for us as we read and reread familiar passages. So we can
expect to be constantly expanding our worship
vocabulary. The important thing is that words and
phrases, new as well as old, should aid our worship and
not make it difficult or mysterious. Toward that end we
want in this chapter to examine the place of language in
our worship practices and also to consider some ways in
which all worshipers can use language more intelligently.

Listening for the Word (John 1:1-5, 9-14)
"In the beginning was the Word." In our attempts to
grasp the full meaning of the language we hear and use

in worship we sometimes confuse the words themselves with "the Word." The beautiful poem that serves as a prologue to John's Gospel speaks of the *Logos,* the creative Word that can be identified with God, the eternal Word that continues to give life and light to all persons. It is this Word that we have come to know and understand in the person of Jesus. Obviously, though John found it necessary to use words in his Gospel, they are certainly subordinate to the everlasting Word, the living truth that can never be contained in any combination of letters from the alphabet.

To add to our confusion, the same term "word" has often been applied to the Bible, which some persons all too quickly identify with the Word of God. The words we read in the scriptures do serve in wonderful ways to bring our minds and hearts into touch with the divine Word, just as they provide our most immediate means of becoming acquainted with Jesus Christ, the incarnate Word. Through the words of the Bible God often speaks quite directly to our hearts. In study and in worship we not only read but listen for the Word of truth and life, even as we listen to the words of ancient and sacred records.

Perhaps, in using and speaking words in worship, what we need most of all to remember is that it is the truths we learn, the lives we touch, the light that falls on our ways, the personal experience we have with Jesus— all these are the realities we seek to discover and not a particular combination of words or a beautiful phrase that speaks to us. Remembering this, we can freely and joyfully make generous use of the treasures of the Bible, which can and should be at the center and core of the language of worship.

Language from the Bible

When Christians worship, the words of the Bible provide a basic support for the language they speak. This is especially evident in Protestant churches that give prominence to the lectern from which the scriptures are read or to the pulpit from which a biblical message is expected. But it is true also in churches that follow some of the ancient liturgies (based on the scriptures) or follow the offices (times of worship) of the day, when psalms are regularly chanted.

Look at your own Sunday services and decide to what extent its language comes from the Bible. Are there designated scripture readings, for individual, for unison, or for responsive use? Consider the call to worship, the invitation to prayer, the sentences before an offering, or the benediction, all of which may be actual quotations or some adaptation of Bible passages.

As we have noted elsewhere in this study, many of our English hymns developed as metrical translations of psalms; but many more in a less direct way use concepts and verbal images, sometimes whole phrases that come from the scriptures. The same observation can be made regarding the prayers that we pray, whether they are carefully composed to reflect biblical patterns of prayer, or whether they come spontaneously to our lips when we feel like expressing our thanksgiving or making our petitions to God. Perhaps more than most musicians realize, the musical settings for our anthems bear witness to a composer's respect for the written text, which music can follow in matters of rhythm and in the mood that the words suggest.

The familiarity of words from the Bible contributes to their value for us in worship. But sometimes that familiarity is a handicap as well. The words drone on as we have always heard them, and they lull us to sleep when we should be listening to some new voice in the Word. But familiarity need not breed disinterest. In worship settings, especially when the Bible can be read aloud, it is possible to hear a familiar passage in a new way, as if you had never heard it before. To discover how exciting the public reading of the Bible can be, read Neh. 8:1-8. The secret of public reading is mostly with the reader, but it is also partly with the listener. Just stop to consider that God is speaking at this moment in the words you hear—and you may suddenly respond to the living Word.

If the words themselves get in the way, consider the value of a paraphrase of the scriptures. Though not as accurate or dependable in a literal way as other translations, a paraphrase can suddenly turn your careless hearing into alert listening to what God is saying to you. You need not wait until a pastor or worship leader provides a paraphrase. Make your own. Take a familiar verse and put its meaning into your own words.

Affirmations of faith

Apart from the reading of the scriptures there are several important ways in which language aids our worship. Historically the church has from time to time formulated statements of its belief that have been recited as creeds, usually as part of a worship service. Unfortunately, such statements have also been utilized as tests of faith, as instruments to brand certain persons as heretics or to deny communion to those who were rejected. In such cases the universal truths that were affirmed in the creeds themselves were forgotten in the arguments over differences of interpretation. Therefore certain religious groups like the Church of the Brethren have refused to require adherence to a creed as a basis for membership. And creeds have not normally been included in our worship services.

Yet there are occasions when congregations could appropriately use one of the great creeds or confessions as a verbal affirmation of our common Christian faith. Some of us are indeed moved when we hear a choir sing portions of the "Credo" that celebrate the life and death and resurrection of Jesus Christ. In recent years some confessions have attempted to translate these same affirmations into language that belongs to our time. Surely there is no reason why any worshiper, if moved to do so, should not write his own confession and be ready to share it with others.

Litanies of praise and prayer

We find more opportunities to join our voices in a verbal expression we call a "litany." This is a form of prayer arranged in a series of supplications and responses. Though the forms of litanies vary, normally a worship leader reads a series of statements or specific prayers or praises, each of which is followed by a shorter response by the congregation. Usually the responses follow a similar pattern and contain much repetition.

The use of typed or printed orders of worship makes it convenient to include litanies in regular services. They are especially suitable for prayers that relate to specific circumstances or conditions in the life of the fellowship. The responses may be read in unison or sung. It is possible, in a quite informal way, to develop a litany without previous rehearsal involving a congregation. A leader may simply suggest that everyone present join in a sung or spoken response, such as "For this we thank you, God." Individuals may feel free to share some reason for joy, each one to be affirmed and supported by the group response.

The sermon as worship
Judging by the way some services of worship have been planned, the sequence of events points to a climax—the sermon. The topic of the message determines the readings and the choice of hymns. The service moves step by step through all the "preliminaries"—and the high moment comes when the preacher mounts the pulpit ("three feet above contradiction," according to one observer) and launches into the discourse of the day. Obviously in many such instances the sermon, what the preacher had to say, is the prime attraction, the reason for meeting. And no one can quarrel with the power that some orators have shown, or the brilliance with which some have expounded "the Word."

But congregational worship requires far more than an audience to hear a speaker. There must be opportunities for praise and petition, for thanksgiving and commitment beyond sitting still and listening. For a preacher to monopolize the use of language in worship is just as harmful as for a priest to control every way of access into the presence of God. The sermon can continue to instruct and inspire, even to exhort to action, while it contributes to a participatory meeting. And one can listen to sermons often in ways that are worshipful.

It is important, for congregations as well as pastors, to think of the sermon as an act of worship, an offering to be counted with other gifts, a means of encouragement, and an aid to worship. Hopefully, the service itself may be planned in such a way that there are creative opportunities, by words or action, to respond to a sermon.

Using words to the glory of God

Language can be a servant rather than a tyrant, but words must be used wisely if they are to aid communication between worshipers and help to interpret the acts of God. Following are a few guidelines that can help us use language to the glory of God and for the good of all.

1. Use language with respect for the words themselves, choosing them carefully for their accuracy and beauty, and for the witness they bear to the eternal Word, the truth expressed in Jesus Christ. One does not have to be either a literary expert or a specialist in matters of style to appreciate that words can hurt as well as heal. If we are thoughtless in our speech, we can harm when we intend to help. The writers of the scriptures were often persons of action rather than scholars, yet they wrote with such vividness and such attention to the vision they saw that their words continue to guide us into the ways of truth.

2. Remember that words can *suggest* as well as *define*. Sometimes we are disturbed by the language of worship because we expect words to be exact and consistent, always meaning just one thing. But words carry overtones of associations and memories. They touch our feelings as well as our thinking. The same word may actually communicate one impression to one worshiper, a different feeling to another. But this should enrich our worship, in that language can suggest mysteries that cannot be defined. Words can evoke an atmosphere that helps us feel the "presence" of God and the "presence" of others who are also part of the body of Christ.

3. Let words bring us face-to-face with God and face-to-face with each other. So often we use language only in the third person—reading about a third party who may or may not be with us. In worship it is never enough to talk about God, as if God were somewhere else. It is far better for the first person—"I" or "we"—to speak directly to a second person—"you." There is a different relationship involved in my speaking to you than in my talking about you. So there is a difference, even in corporate worship, when the words we use are face-to-face words, person-to-person words. Notice how Psalm 23 begins by speaking in image words about the Lord as our shepherd. But after a few phrases in which the good shepherd is always "he," the relationship changes, and the psalmist cries out *"Thou* art with me." What was a description suddenly becomes a declaration of praise, a personal testimony. So it is always with the face-to-face quality of the language of prayers.

4. The words we use in worship should be as inclusive as possible. If we speak for our brothers and sisters, let us make sure we use words that count them in—and do not exclude them. This is one of the problems some people have with many of the biblical images that are common in the language of worship. Words like "Lord" and "King," for example, recall a time when most persons were subjects of rulers—nearly always men—and were expected to obey without question. In this day we do not so honor kings, yet royal images run through our Christmas language and our great choruses of praise on almost any Sunday. We do not need to discard all traditional images. We can cherish their beauty and learn from them; but we may need to encourage the use of other images that grow out of our own time. It is not a matter of rejecting old phrases, but of being sensitive to other ways of speaking that can include all persons.

Especially do we need to be sensitive to the feelings of women worshipers who tell us frankly that so many of the terms we use (even many of the words applied to God) and so many of the hymns we sing make them feel left out. This was not, of course, the intention of biblical writers or of hymn writers. We may have quite different ideas about the need to change familiar expressions, but we should encourage efforts in new hymns and songs and in new liturgies, even in the prayers we pray and the comments we make, to use inclusive language wherever possible. At first the effort may seem a little awkward, but we can soon grow accustomed to worship language that celebrates what Paul affirmed in Gal. 3:28, "There is neither Jew nor Greek, there is neither slave nor free, there is neither male nor female, for you are all one in Christ Jesus."

5. Words find their highest destiny when, like the eternal Word of John's prologue, they become incarnated in persons and in deeds. If words can lead to action, they can indeed "become flesh" and "dwell among us." The language of worship often is poetic language, full of rhythm and music and a beauty all its own. But such language fails to glorify God if it becomes an end in itself, something merely to enjoy aesthetically. Our worship words should move us toward commitment and dedication, pushing us beyond the walls of our churches and into the world to serve, so that, like Isaiah on hearing the call of God, we reply, "Send me."

9
Raise a Joyful Song: Music in Worship

Break into songs of joy, sing psalms.
Sing psalms in the Lord's honour with the harp,
with the harp and with the music of the psaltery.
                                        Ps. 98:4-5 (NEB)

You don't sing? And you can't carry a tune? That's hard to believe because you've been making music from the day you were born. That first cry was a sustained sound, with a tone all its own. Your mother and father heard music in the cooing, gurgling noises you made before you could talk. And there was a beat in your pulse from that first day on. Often you would call for Mom-mie or Dad-dy with an accent on the first syllable and with a high note followed by a low one, or sometimes, in anger, the other way around.

Music began for you when you were able to sustain a sound, form a tone, use your natural sense of rhythm (as regular as a heartbeat) and develop little melodies in cadences that are still a part of your speech. You may even have harmonized with another voice. All the elements are there—even if you can't read a note of music and think your voice is a monotone.

Music in worship is just as natural, just as interwoven

with all the various ways in which we express our
thanksgiving and praise, make our petitions and prayers,
or reach out to touch other persons in the body of
Christ. Music is integral to worship and celebration. It
may serve as a means or a tool to implement acts of
praise, but music is far more than an aid. It is a gift we
offer with ourselves when we sense the presence of God.

Music and the church—a partnership
If we had some convenient way of arranging in parallel
columns a summary history of music and a summary
history of religion, we would be amazed to discover how
interrelated they are. One history of music, for example,
begins its study of the origins of western music with a
section on the birth of the Christian church. And similar
parallels could be noted in more ancient times, not only
among the Hebrews whose music was often described in
the Old Testament, but among pagan peoples as well,
where temple observances required music, and cultic
practices called for singers and dancers.

The scope of this chapter allows hardly more than a
mention of the history of sacred music, either the
ceremonial developments within the church, or the
schools of music that churches provided, or the encouragement that Christian institutions gave to composers and performers. We can simply observe that our
concerts today would be impoverished, our treasures in
recordings would be vastly diminished, and music itself
would lose· much of its universal appeal if we had no
heritage of sacred music or of music created by and for
the Christian church.

The church's own worship would be even more handicapped if we should be deprived of music as a gift, of
music as a heritage, of music as an expression of what a
congregation contributes to worship. In order to appreciate all that sacred music offers, let us look
specifically at the treasures that are immediately at hand
in the hymns we sing, hymns that in a limited way introduce us to the songs of Christians across many centuries and in several continents, while at the same time

they serve the immediate need we have for expressions of our prayer and praise.

Following is a selection of fourteen hymns, available in most standard hymnals, that illustrate the musical resources we can utilize at any service. As you read some of the stanzas, hum some of the tunes, or simply observe the origin and background of each, consider the riches of song that are available either for your individual devotion or for corporate worship.

The hymnal's rich heritage of song

"Of the Father's Love Begotten" (116). Between the 5th and the 9th centuries there developed for use with the liturgy of the church a kind of plain chant often called Gregorian after the pope who organized the melodies used by singers. Male voices, singing in unison and without accompaniment, sang the words of psalms and responses to long-flowing melodies. A good example of such music is the tune often used with an early Latin hymn written by Prudentius near the beginning of the 5th century, a hymn in honor of Christ, the source and the ending, begotten of the Father's love.

"Come, Ye Faithful, Raise the Strain" (183). brilliant writer, John of Damascus, who gave up wealth to live in a cave-like monastery in Judea, may have done for the eastern church in the eighth century what Pope Gregory had done for the west a century before. Our hymnals do not reflect his contribution to music but they do include a few of his hymns that we sing at Easter. John adapted choral music to church use and wrote a series of "canons," long poems of many stanzas from which we have this story "of triumphant gladness."

"Jesus, the Very Thought of Thee" (109). Latin hymns and priestly chants may seem as foreign to our worship as a towering cathedral differs from our meetingplaces. Yet some of the hymns of devotion we cherish most originated in just such a setting. The time is the 12th century, the place is France, the hymnwriter is a monk, Bernard of Clairvaux, the head of a monastic order and a powerful force in the church. From a long hymn he wrote on the name of Jesus several hymns have been translated into English and still have a place in our worship, such as "Jesus the Very Thought of Thee," and "Jesus, Thou Joy of Loving Hearts" (202).

"The Strife Is O'er, the Battle Done" (190). While Martin Luther and John Calvin were calling for reforms in the Roman church, an Italian composer, called Palestrina after his birthplace, was helping to reform the music in the church, making it more suitable for worship. Choirs still sing his motets and anthems with their beautiful interweaving melodies. His contribution to our hymnals is a song of victory most often sung at Easter.

"A Mighty Fortress Is Our God" (75) Every church musician should offer a special prayer of thanks that so influential a reformer as Martin Luther composed music and believed it should have a central place in worship. He insisted also that church musicians should have adequate income, and he wanted congregations to participate more fully in singing, even if this involved using some of the folk tunes they already knew. Thanks to Luther the German chorale has a prominent place in our services. And our hymnals include several of his own hymns, the best known of which is "A Mighty Fortress," often called the "battle hymn of the Reformation."

"All People That on Earth Do Dwell" (2). John Calvin did not share Luther's enthusiasm about music. In the Reformed churches over which he had control only psalms could be sung (in metrical translations from the Hebrew). There could be no part-singing and no instruments. But fortunately some of the psalms were set to good solid tunes by Louis Bourgeois, whose tunes found their way to England and eventually to America, especially the one called "Old Hundreth" because it went with Psalm 100.

"The Lord's My Shepherd" (273). Hebrew poetry has long-flowing phrases with many image words. It doesn't often fit easily into the short lines and strict meters of English hymns. One of the most successful of these "metrical psalms" that Puritans brought with them to America is this arrangement of Psalm 23.

"When I Survey the Wondrous Cross" (174). At first almost all English hymns were limited to psalms. Then, after a struggle, churches were willing to use "spiritual songs" like this devotional hymn by Isaac Watts that Christians everywhere join in singing. It is most effective when sung to a tune taken from the old Gregorian chant, arranged by Lowell Mason.

"Amazing Grace" (433). Folk melodies, both in Europe and America, have provided some of the best settings for familiar hymns. Recently, popular music performers discovered a hymn tune long beloved by Americans. They still sing it with John Newton's tribute to grace that "brought me safe thus far," and "will lead me home."

"God of Grace and God of Glory" (321). Only in Wales could one expect to find annual festivals devoted to contests between community choruses singing hymns that accompany native melodies. Several of these tunes are in your hymnal, the most popular being "Cwm Rhondda." Fortunately we can sing the Welsh tunes without having to pronounce their Welsh names. A contemporary text to sing with this tune is "God of Grace and God of Glory."

"Steal Away" (487). Negro spirituals are genuine folk hymns from our own history, many of them rich in devotional meaning as well as memorable for singing. Like other music that developed among people who could not read, the spirituals usually include a simple refrain that anyone can learn quickly, to be sung in response to a solo voice.

"Lo, a Gleam From Yonder Heaven" (454). The heritage of sacred music belongs to all Christians, and we are ecumenical in the way we share the songs of many centuries and different traditions. Yet we also value hymns that have been written within our own household of faith. Brethren love the hymns of William Beery, especially the one with words written by his wife.

"They'll Know We Are Christians by Our Love" (No. 6 in *The Brethren Songbook*). Each generation produces new songwriters, new musicians, and new ways of praising the Lord in music. So hymnals and songbooks need often to be revised or replaced or supplemented with new songs. Some of the more recent have the feeling of folk music, and they are often sung in unison. They may lack some of the stateliness of older hymns, but they are still effective in worship especially when they express basic convictions and help worshipers affirm their participation in the body of Christ.

Response-ability

To join in singing hymns is not the only way members of a congregation share in a ministry of music. In many services, following a practice that comes from the earliest churches, worshipers have a significant part in singing or repeating simple responses. They may appear in a kind of conversation between the minister or worship leader and the people. Or the congregation's part may simply be to speak or sing a "hallelujah"—as did Hebrew worshipers—or an enthusiastic "amen."

Your hymnal can assist you in singing responses since many have been set to simple tunes. There is no reason why this aspect of church praise should be left only to choirs or individual voices. Take time to study the resources your own hymnal offers by way of musical worship aids that are appropriate for almost every part in the sequence of a service. (In *The Brethren Hymnal* these resources are numbered from 615 to 693). Perhaps it will be helpful to note the importance of several of their typical responses:

Invocation. An invocation is a prayer that asks God to be present, to hear, to bless, and to guide, usually at the beginning of a service.

Call to Worship. Not a prayer, but a statement and an invitation that helps a congregation prepare for worship. Some are taken directly from the Bible, such as Psalm 95:6; Isa. 55:6; or Heb. 2:20.

Doxology. Perhaps the most familiar formula of praise to God as Father, Son, and Holy Ghost. It is appropriate for many occasions, not only when an offering is presented.

Te Deum Laudamus. Some portions of an ancient Latin hymn which begins "We praise thee, O God," are often used as a choral response.

Gloria Patri. Another familiar doxology comes from the second century. It was originally a teaching hymn, but it is quite commonly used as a response, beginning "Glory be to the Father."

Sanctus. "Holy, Holy, Holy" is the first line of a familiar hymn. These are also the words, taken from Isaiah 6:3, of a response, that celebrates the goodness and holiness of God.

Kyrie Eleison. These are Greek words for a short petition that simply means, "Lord, have mercy on us."

Hosanna in Excelsis. "Hosanna in the highest" was the cry of the crowds who welcomed Jesus to Jerusalem (Matt. 21:8-9).

Gloria in Excelsis Deo. "Glory to God in the highest" was the song of the "heavenly host" who announced the birth of Jesus (Luke 2:14). It was also an ancient Christian hymn.

Our Father. The Lord's Prayer—or Disciples' Prayer—continues to have a central place in many services of worship. Most often spoken, it can also be sung, either as a chant or to a familiar musical setting.

Antiphon. From the practice of Hebrew worshipers in the temple and synagogue, Christians have learned an effective way of praying and singing—antiphonally, with two groups responding to each other, sometimes repeating, sometimes answering the other. Certain responses are called antiphons, arranged so that a leader and a congregation, or a choir and congregation can be in worshipful conversation, one responding to the other. Words of scripture, verses of hymns, or original material may be included either to be read or sung.

Benediction. A benediction is a closing sentence or prayer that does not necessarily need to be "pronounced" by a minister but may at times be sung as well as prayed in unison by the congregation.

Amen. What the word means is simply "so be it." The amen may be an ending for a hymn or prayer, spoken or sung. Some choral amens may be threefold, fourfold, even sevenfold, but others are quite simple. It is an expression that belongs not only to ministers and singers, but to every worshiper.

Your share in music celebration

1. Whatever may be the extent of your participation in music—as a listener, as a singer, as a leader, as an accompanist, or as one who only joins in familiar refrains—remember that you contribute to an act of worship and praise. You are more than an audience, and your voice is needed.

2. You can sing or play or listen to the glory of God. Hardly any musician today can match the scope and brilliance, the finesse and comprehensiveness of Johann Sebastian Bach in either instrumental or choral composition, yet this master of church music dedicated his compositions *Soli Dei Gloria,* "for the glory of God alone." Lacking any such talent, you can make the same dedication "as you sing . . . in your hearts to God" (Col. 3:16-17).

3. You can sing with the spirit—and with understanding. Music provides a means of emotional expression, and many worshipers rightly find a kind of freedom in song to express their feelings of joy and exultation. Yet even when the spirit takes over, a worshiper dare not forget the presence of others in the body of the church. Each of us in moments of ecstasy needs the restraining word of Paul who put it so well when counseled the Corinthian church, "I will sing with the spirit, and I will sing with the mind also" (1 Cor. 14:13-18). We can make music in a way that edifies and informs our brothers and sisters. Let your mind sing along when your heart is beating time.

4. You can "sing to the Lord a new song." God is still at work, and it will require new songs if God's activity is to be properly celebrated. Granted—the old familiar hymns are the ones you remember best and sing most readily. But they too were once new and not at all familiar. Suppose the first Christians, remembering the

Hebrew songs of Zion, had said, "Please, nothing new." How would we have learned to celebrate the resurrection? Suppose that Martin Luther, devoted to the Bible, had ruled out any new hymns. Where would we have learned his "Mighty Fortress"? Or, without risking some new songs, how could Christians ever have listened to Isaac Watts, or Charles Wesley, or William Beery, or the haunting echoes of Negro spirituals? Be daring. Try some new songs to mix with the old.

5. Listen to the songs of other generations. Our tastes in music vary with the years and our mixed experiences. Yet our heritage of sacred music is itself a mixture of plainsong, folksong, dance tunes, along with the music of great composers. New forms of worship may at first disturb us by their strangeness. They may not be "our" music, but they are someone's praise. At least we can respectfully listen and perhaps thereby receive a blessing.

6. You can enjoy great choral music even if you never sing. There are dozens of oratorios and cantatas—works like *Elijah, The Creation* or *The Messiah*—that do more than some of our Bible lessons to instruct us in the drama and the power of the Christian faith, simply because music has been employed to underline and interpret the Bible message. Not as concertgoers, but as worshipers we can approach the rich treasures of choral music and grow in our appreciation of the music of praise.

7. Let music itself be an offering you bring to God. We are mistaken if we think of music only as background, or atmosphere, or as a way of filling time while people assemble for worship, or as a means of paving the way for a sermon. Music is a part of what we bring to worship and praise, not an accessory but a gift that is worthy of our presenting it, along with our hearts to God.

10
Images of the Invisible: Signs and Symbols

Now we see only puzzling reflections in a mirror, but then we shall see face to face. My knowledge now is partial, then it will be whole. 1 Cor. 13:12 (NEB)

The simple, frame church seemed almost barren in its plainness. But someone had placed a table in the front between the congregation's chairs and the low platform where the minister and the worship leader sat. The leader reminded the congregation that each one had been invited to place some object on the table, something that was individual and personal, something that signified what that person believed in, or worked for, or valued greatly.

As the people brought their contributions, one or two at a time, the worship leader arranged them on the table. The minister took that opportunity to note Bible passages that were related to some of the gifts. The objects began to cover the table. Some were conventional, like the Bible, a hymnal, or a baptismal certificate. Others reflected vocational interests, like a stethoscope, a hammer, or a computer. Still others were unexpected: a loaf of bread, a toy, an original painting, a baseball, a fish hook, a road map, an airline schedule, and a 20-year-old wedding picture.

As the service proceeded there were readings from the Bible, stanzas of hymns, and short statements by members who explained why some things they carried so easily in their hands were still so important to them. In each case the object itself was only a sign pointing to something that was vital and real, yet something difficult to explain. For their concluding ceremony they joined hands around the table that now represented so much of their lives. The leader thanked God for symbols of everyday life that point to faith and hope and love. Even the circle they formed was a symbol of their unity as members of Christ's body, the church.

Many of the important experiences in our lives are difficult to explain in words because they involve relationships with God or with other persons. Or they may deal with concepts—like love and trust, or faith and forgiveness—that may be rather abstract. So we turn to symbols for help in expressing ourselves. Something that everyone knows—a tree, a star, a shepherd guarding his sheep, a mother caring for her children—these are the pictures we can use to suggest what we mean. It is obvious that Christian worship must utilize symbols regularly to signify the presence of God, to demonstrate the way God's Spirit continues to move among us, and to celebrate the reality of the support and strength we find in the Christian community.

In our study of signs and symbols it may be helpful to observe that through the years Christians have used three basic kinds of symbols in their worship. Some of these are essentially verbal, others are in the form of actions or movements, and many more are made vivid to us because they are visual.

Verbal symbols

If you were asked to explain in just a few words what it means for you to trust God, you might use theological terms that you heard somewhere, but more likely you would say, "It's like reaching up and taking the hand of a friend who knows the way." Or you might compare God to a shepherd, a pilot, someone whose strong arms would never let you fall. You would turn to picture words, figures of speech. Or you might tell a story.

So it has been through the years. The Bible is filled with narratives, poems, and parables. Its pages contain countless image words that have become a part of our own speech. The Hebrew people took seriously the commandment "You shall make no graven images." Instead of attempting to picture God or carving an idol—even God's name was sacred—they turned to image words. Their storytellers would speak of a ladder reaching to heaven, a burning bush, the rushing of a mighty wind, or a still small voice. And their poets would sing of God as a refuge, a light, a king, a shepherd, a judge, or a loving parent who is concerned for every son and daughter.

Note how natural it is to think of Jesus as the good shepherd. This is due largely to verbal images that have come to us through our acquaintance with Psalm 23, which pictures God as one who guards, provides, protects, disciplines, and saves. Therefore in our minds we think of Jesus as a shepherd who loves his sheep, directing them into good pastures. Jesus used the same figure of speech, the same set of verbal symbols, to observe that the good shepherd knows his sheep, and will even give his own life voluntarily to save them (John 10:1-18). In one of his parables Jesus compares God's love for a lost person to a good shepherd's efforts to save one lost sheep (Luke 15:3-7).

You can understand why the early Christians, when they turned eventually to forming pictures, whether in words or in stone, to signify their faith, could so readily take a common pagan symbol of their time, the shepherd carrying his sheep across his shoulders, and make it their own. This symbol soon came to represent Jesus, their own good shepherd.

Action symbols
Although Jesus frequently used parables, picture stories, to make clear the point of his teachings, perhaps his greatest contribution to giving us helpful symbols was not in the words he spoke as much as in what he did.

This was particularly true in the concluding events of his ministry, as he looked forward to his approaching death on the cross and sought for ways to help his followers understand the meaning of what was about to happen. It seems also that he was eager to show by significant actions how it would be possible for them to continue his ministry and to become more bold and aggressive in their witness.

At the time of the Lord's Supper, Jesus did a surprising thing when he washed his disciples' feet. Perhaps more than anything he might have said concerning their need for cleansing and the importance of service was his own action in a physical way as he knelt with basin and towel. What he did was to be more than a gesture. John 13 indicates that he intended his example to be followed. The Church of the Brethren is one of just a few Christian groups who have taken these instructions seriously, developing a ritual closely patterned on Jesus' action in the upper room. Not only has our practice enriched our teaching about humility and service; it has also helped us to carry the meaning of our worship over into experiences of daily life when we, as Christians, find many opportunities to "wash the feet of the world."

On the same occasion Jesus took two very common and ordinary parts of the supper and pointed out how their own breaking of bread and eating the bread together and their drinking from a common cup could be regarded as memorials, also symbols, of his life and death, and especially of his giving of himself on their behalf. Certainly the most effective symbols are those which are common to our everyday experiences. Can you think of anything more essential to basic living than eating bread? An action so common that it was a part of every meal—that is what Jesus took as a universal symbol, one that various Christian traditions in the years since have celebrated, even as our symbolic actions are patterned upon the actions of Jesus.

Certainly one of the obvious values of action symbols is that they can be often repeated, imitated perhaps, or at least incarnated in actions that help us put our beliefs and our worship ceremonies into the form of deeds.

Visual symbols

Many of the rich treasures that we today associate with our western civilization and culture incorporate visual symbols that through the years have been meaningful to Christians as ways of pointing to their beliefs and as ways of teaching Christian truths. On your visit to an art gallery you may be quickly impressed with the surprising amount of Christian symbolism you find in paintings and in sculptures. Some of the symbols appear in connection with objects that were originally designed for ritual use in church or as part of the decoration that went into the building of a giant cathedral. Especially during the centuries when most people could not read or write, the visual symbols they could observe in mosaics, in stained glass windows, in the sculpture that appeared on their churches, or in the furniture and vessels that were used in their church services—all of these became ways by which Christian truths and even the vast range of stories from the Bible could be taught to them.

Let us take just one example of a visual symbol that seems to be used almost universally as the central Christian symbol. Strange as it may seen, the cross was not one of the symbols used by Christians in the first two centuries after the time of Christ. Even though the emphasis upon the cross, and the teaching regarding Christ crucified, was so central in the letters of Paul and elsewhere in the New Testament, the early worship experiences of Christians centered more on the joy they experienced in the resurrection. It was not really until the fourth century that the cross began to be important as a symbol to be placed at the center of the Christian faith and to be given great prominence in Christian worship.

Originally the cross suggested a means of execution for slaves or an instrument of torture and suffering. Obviously it was a mark of disgrace and defeat, a burden to be carried or a load to be lifted. In writing to the Corinthian church Paul observed that the preaching of the cross was a stumbling block to proud people such as the

Jews who did not see in it, as Paul did, a sign of the
power of God. Paul recognized that in Christ what
seemed to be weakness was stronger than any other
human power. In the same way Paul also noted that for
a reasonable people like the Greeks, who were constantly
seeking wisdom, the fact of Christ being crucified, would
appear as a sign of folly, or sheer nonsense. Yet to Paul
what people regarded as foolishness could really represent the wisdom of God.

During all the centuries that the cross has received
such a prominent place in Christian worship, its meaning
has remained paradoxical and puzzling to many. But as a
symbol it continues to call attention to the whole
ministry of Jesus as the suffering servant, who gave his
life for all persons everywhere. It is certainly one of the
most effective visual symbols, and it deserves the central
place it has in Christian art and literature.

Values and limitations of symbols
Symbols in various forms can be effective instruments in
enriching our worship, in strengthening our teaching,
and in illuminating our daily experiences. But we need
also to note that there are limitations to their use, and
there may even be dangers in their misuse. It is so easy
for a symbol, whether in words, or deeds, or in pictures,
to be substituted for the important value it represents.
Sometimes symbols, when they are incorporated into
works of art, can become an object of worship in
themselves. Or they may be regarded as having magical
powers, so that a worshiper is tempted to use them as
pagans used to turn to a fetish or an idol. It is possible to
be very legalistic about the observance of an ordinance
like the feetwashing service, and yet to overlook how
such a basic activity must be demonstrated in contemporary acts of service. It is easy for ministers and
teachers to take the picture words that are used in the
Bible and to twist them and turn them in order to make
some point that would be far from the intention of the
biblical writer.

But if symbols are properly understood as means

toward understanding and not as ends in themselves, they most certainly have an important place in Christian worship.

A listing of common Christian symbols

1. Fish. One of the earliest symbols that Christians used in pointing to Jesus was the fish. It may have served as a secret sign for Christians in danger of persecution since its meaning came from an acrostic. The Greek word for fish is *ichthus,* composed of the initial letter for five words, "Jesus Christ, God's Son, Savior." Since fish are at home in water, some Christians see them as symbols of baptism. Others think of the loaves and fish that fed five thousand people (John 6:1-14) and of the early disciples who were called to be "fishers of men" (Matt. 4:19). Fig. A.

2. Anchor. The writer of the epistle to the Hebrews describes the hope that Christians have to "a sure and steadfast anchor of the soul" (Heb. 6:19-20). As a symbol of faith the anchor took on even greater meaning when it was developed as an early form of the cross. Fig. B.

3. Dove. For Hebrew worshipers the dove was a symbol of peace (Genesis 8:6-12) and an offering for purification (Luke 2:24). But Christians also regard the dove as symbolic of the coming of the Holy Spirit, as on the occasion of Jesus' baptism (John 1:32). In religious art a descending dove often suggests the coming of the Spirit. Fig. C.

4. Crown. As a mark of victory or ruling authority, a crown may symbolize Jesus as king. A crown of thorns refers rather to his sacrificial death when he was mockingly hailed as "king of the Jews" (Mark 15:16-18). The crown may also signify the reward for a faithful life (1 Peter 5:4). Fig. D.

5. Hand. Because the Old Testament opposed the making of graven images of the deity, the Hebrews did not attempt to depict God's countenance. Early Christian art, however, suggested the presence and power of God by a hand that issued from a cloud. There are many references in the Bible to the hand of God (Ex. 15:6;

Josh. 4:24; Ps. 48:10; Ps. 139:10; Prov. 1:24; Eccles. 9:1; Acts 7:55; 1 Peter 5:6). In recent years the symbolism of clasped hands has served to represent friendship and close relationship. Albrecht Durer's drawing of "praying hands" has become an eloquent symbol of private devotion. Fig. E.

6. *Lamb.* When John the Baptist saw Jesus coming toward him, he said, "Behold the lamb of God" (John 1:29). The lamb of God (*Angus Dei* in Latin) is an early symbol of Christ, sometimes pictured with a banner, suggesting his victory over death. But when Jesus is represented as the good shepherd, the lamb he carries refers to the ones he rescues. Fig. F.

7. *Wheat or bread.* So necessary is bread for sustaining life that it almost universally represents food and nourishment. A loaf may symbolize the life of Jesus (John 6:35). Broken, it may refer to his comments regarding his death and the familiar communion symbol (Luke 22:19; 1 Cor. 11:23-24). Often a sheaf of wheat may call attention to "the bread of life." Fig. G.

8. *Cup or chalice.* At the Lord's Supper, Jesus probably used a simple drinking cup. His comments regarding drinking his cup (Matt. 20:22-23; 26:27-29; Luke 22:17-18) suggest that it be regarded as a symbol of his own lifeblood. Its central importance in the earliest observances of the Lord's Supper is indicated by Paul (1 Cor. 11:25-29). The oldest known chalice, a cup used in liturgical services, is the chalice of Antioch, discovered in 1910 but of ancient origin. A cup with a different symbolic meaning, representing fellowship and service (Mark 9:41), is the Brethren Service cup, widely used in Brethren churches during and following World War II. Fig. H.

9. *Vine or grapes.* The vine is an emblem of Jesus (John 15:1, 5, 8). It points to the living relationship between him and his disciples and to their responsibility for fruitbearing. But grapes, the fruit of the vine, also symbolize the blood of Christ and the cup of the new covenant (Luke 22:17-18; 1 Cor. 11:25). Fig. I.

10. *Tree.* Trees may represent either life or death in

Fig. A

Fig. B

Fig. C

Fig. D

Fig. E

Fig. F

Fig. G

Fig. H

Fig. I

Fig. J

Fig. K

Fig. L

Fig. M

Fig. N

Fig. O

Fig. P

Christian symbolism, depending upon the context. Certain trees in Eden had a specific character (Genesis 2). Other trees mentioned in the Bible were associated with particular qualities: the cedar with growth (Ps. 92:12), the mustard tree with faith in small beginnings (Matt. 13:31-32), the olive tree with peace and deliverance (Gen. 8:10-11), and the palm tree with victory (John 12:12-15). But the New Testament also refers to the cross as a tree (Acts 5:30). Fig. J.

11. *Tongues of fire.* Fire and flame are most often associated with the presence of the Holy Spirit, as at Pentecost (Acts 2:1-4). Or they may refer to the various gifts of the Spirit. Fig. K.

12. *Alpha and Omega.* A number of Greek letters are used as symbols, especially Chi Rho, the first two letters of the Greek name for Christ, and the first and last letters of the Greek alphabet, Alpha and Omega, which the book of Revelation (22:13) identifies with Christ, the beginning and the end. Fig. L.

13. *Open book.* Several familiar symbols call attention to the Bible or portions of it. An open book suggests the availability of the scriptures. Tables of stone refer more specifically to the law, especially the Ten Commandments. A lamp or a torch may also signify the light that comes from the Word of God (Psalm 119:105). Fig. M.

14. *Trinity.* Belief in God as Father, Son, and Holy Spirit has been central to the Christian faith since New Testament times. Although the Bible offers verbal statements and formulas supporting the doctrine of the Trinity, the symbols that Christians use have been drawn not from scripture but from other sources, like an equilateral triangle, a three-leafed flower, three interlocking circles, or some other design. Fig. N.

15. *Basin and towel.* It is strange that a New Testament symbol of cleansing and service (John 13:1-5), one that Jesus deliberately introduced as an example for all, should appear so seldom in Christian art and symbolism. In recent years Brethren have recognized its value, not only as an action symbol to be perpetrated in an or-

dinance but also as a graphic visual symbol representing service. Fig. O.

16. *The resurrection.* Although the resurrection of Christ remains the central affirmation of faith among Christians, the symbols most commonly chosen to represent it come not from the New Testament but from legendary sources and natural objects. The lily is a symbol both of purity and of new life; the pomegranate suggests the hope of new life through the scattering of many seeds; the phoenix was a legendary creature that rose up from the ashes of its own burning; the peacock grows new feathers more beautiful than the ones it loses; and the butterfly sheds its cocoon to fly away with a new body and beautiful wings. Fig. P.

11
Where God Dwells: A Place of Meeting

Even the sparrow finds a home,
and the swallow a nest for herself
where she may lay her young,
at thy altars, O Lord of hosts . . .
Blessed are those who dwell in thy house,
ever singing thy praise! Ps. 84:3-4 (RSV)

The great west door of St. Paul's Cathedral in London swung open to admit a colorful and stately procession. The year was 1958, and all the bishops of the Anglican communion, more than 300 of them from around the world, were on hand for the beginning of their Lambeth conference, held once every ten years.

I watched as the verger and crossbearer led the procession of bishops robed in red and white, followed by the choir, the primates and metropolitans, finally by the Archbishop of Canterbury—all moving to the front of the nave to stand before the high altar. Such an occasion must have been in the mind of the architect, Sir Christopher Wren, when he designed a church so rich in symbolism, gleaming in glass and stone, in wood and metal, topped by a dome that would dominate the London skyline.

Just a few weeks later that same summer I attended another convocation, composed this time mostly of a few hundred Americans who had come to Schwarzenau in Germany to join with German friends there on the 250th anniversary of the beginning of the Church of the Brethren. Perhaps it was appropriate that, of the three major services then, two were held in a tent provided alongside the Alexander Mack School in the village, the other on the banks of the river Eder where the initial service of baptism of eight persons launched the new church.

There were some church dignitaries at Schwarzenau: Bishop Ernst Wilm of the Evangelical Church in Germany, Dr. W. A. Visser't Hooft, then secretary of the World Council of Churches, as well as Brethren officials. And there were printed orders of service in both German and English. But somehow the occasion did not require a vast sanctuary with stained-glass windows. The temporary tent, the soft sunlight, the view of tree-lined mountains, and the quiet movement of the stream nearby—all of these contributed to an awareness of God's presence and a tie with a past day when some Christians separated themselves from their imposing church buildings to seek for a deeper sense of God's dwelling in a community of believers.

Where God dwells
A place set apart for worship—must it have some distinctive marks that designate it as a special place, a holy place? Must it assert itself over other places so that it can be seen from afar? Must it always be close to the daily life of a congregation? Or is the congregation of believers itself the dwellingplace of God?

The answers are not simple, and worshipers have differed since earliest times. Given a vision of God, Jacob took the stone that was his pillow and set it up for a pillar, believing at that moment that "this is none other than the house of God" (Gen. 28:10-22). Years later Moses provided a "tent of meeting" outside the camp of the people of Israel "to which they might go to seek the

Lord" (Ex. 33:7-11). But soon there was need for a more permanent, lavishly decorated tabernacle which would be filled with the glory of the Lord (Ex. 39:32-43; 40). And there was great rejoicing indeed when Solomon, having erected a great central temple in Jerusalem, could say, "I have built thee an exalted house, a place for thee to dwell in forever" (1 Kings 6: 8:12-30).

So it must have been disturbing to persons cherishing such an exalted house for God to observe the drastic way in which Jesus "cleansed" the temple and to hear him suggest that the temple of his body could replace a building that it took 46 years to construct (John 2:13-22). Yet there was surely some significance in one of the phenomena that accompanied the crucifixion, when "the curtain of the temple was torn in two, from top to bottom" (Matt. 27:50-54).

An old order of worship had been shaken indeed—and from top to bottom. No longer were faithful believers to require the ministrations of a priest to gain access to the holy of holies, Jesus had said, "Where two or three are gathered in my name, there am I in the midst of them" (Matt. 18:20). And Stephen, in his valedictory sermon, insisted that God "does not dwell in houses made with hands" (Acts 7:44-50). Though the first Christians for a time attended the temple and worshiped in synagogues, either by choice or necessity they soon located their worship in private homes (Acts 2:46-47; Acts 5:12-21, 42). There are numerous references in Paul's letters to house churches and to the individuals who were, in one sense, hosts to the church (1 Cor. 16:19; Rom. 16:23; Col. 4:15). From Paul's perspective, many of the old restraints and separations, often symbolized in the barriers between priest and people, between worshiper and God, were no longer operative since worshipers are "all one in Christ" (Gal. 3:26-28). The writer of the epistle to the Hebrews put it differently: Christians are now to enter the sanctuary "by the new and living way" that Jesus had opened (Heb. 10:19-25).

What buildings serve best for Christian worship? Consider the ways Christians have built for that purpose.

From congregations to buildings

The time came when Christians needed their own places of meeting. Private homes served for a time, especially the more spacious ones in which there would be a vestibule, an open atrium, an assembly room with a small platform, and perhaps also a dining room (for their *agape* meals), and perhaps even a baptistry. Yet in times of persecution in Rome, Christians assembled in catacombs, burial rooms that offered secrecy as well as space for meeting. During the third century other buildings were erected for Christian worship. Yet even in this situation some church leaders said, "it is not the place but the company of the elect" that was to be called the "church." And indeed the words we so easily apply to church buildings were intended at first to designate not a building but a congregation.

The early buildings were modeled after Roman civic buildings used for trade, for courts, and for public assemblies, called "basilicas." At one end there was a semicircular extension called an "apse" where a judge or ruler would sit. As churches became larger in the years when Christianity was officially recognized and encouraged, the role of priests and clergy became more important. It was natural for the priests to take the place of judges. An altar was located in the apse. So church buildings began to reflect not so much a servant church as a triumphant church. And little by little their structures became more complicated with the usual result that the people were again separated from the symbols of God's presence—and more dependent upon priests who guarded a holy place and the holy things associated with it.

Types of church architecture

Through the years several kinds of church architecture have developed, each with certain distinctive characteristics, each reflecting aspects of the culture of the time. Since many of the great churches still stand, some as monuments, but many still as places of worship, and since each style has been copied in churches we still see, it will be helpful to note briefly how these buildings differ.

1. *Byzantine* is a word used to describe the culture that developed mostly in eastern Europe and the Middle East from the fourth century until the Middle Ages. Its first center was called Byzantium, later Constantinople, now Istanbul. Byzantine churches are noted for their domes, raised over round arches or set on a square base. Many of the early churches were circular in shape or in the form of an octagon (Fig. A). In later years Greek and Russian churches would have several domes. Walls were frequently covered by mosaics, sometimes by fresco paintings. Two of the best-known Byzantine churches are St. Sophia in Istanbul, erected in the sixth century (later a mosque and now a museum), and St. Mark's cathedral in Venice, begun in the eleventh century.

2. *Romanesque* is the term applied to buildings erected mostly in western Europe from the fifth to the twelfth centuries that utilized the Roman skill in building round arches. The walls of church buildings, most of them following the plan of the basilica, were quite solid and thick but gradually arches were placed on arches until ceilings could be lofty. In England many Romanesque churches are called Norman. Though beautiful in most cases, some of them suggest a fortress that may be secure but somewhat lacking in sunlight. Fig. B.

3. *Gothic* architecture developed in France in the early Middle Ages as builders discovered ways of providing more window space and greater interior light. Flying buttresses on the outside permitted lofty spaces inside with room for high-reaching stained-glass windows. The pointed arch and the upward-lifting lines of the cathedral seemed to draw the worshiper toward God. These churches were adorned with sculptures that recounted the Bible story for persons who could not read. The design of most Gothic churches, like that of the Romanesque, was in the form of a cross. Fig. C.

4. *Renaissance* churches, as might be expected, recalled some of the classic forms of Greek and Roman buildings. One of the most famous is St. Peter's in Rome

Fig. A

Fig. B

which is both massive and ornate, crowned by the dome that Michelangelo designed, still the largest church in the world (Fig. D). In southern Europe later churches took on the elaborate designs and flowing decorations that we call "baroque."

5. *The Meetinghouse.* When the Protestant reformation swept across many countries in Europe, there was a reaction against practices associated with medieval churches, and some reformers initiated changes that were bound to affect the buildings they had taken over. In many instances the altar was moved forward, closer to the people, where it served as a communion table. The pulpit became more prominent. The elaborate screens that used to divide clergy from laity were taken down. But even so, many of the old medieval buildings, shorn of some of their statuary and symbols, were continued in use.

But the reformers also built churches that were much simpler and plainer. They put a pulpit in the center near the front, facing the congregation which had become an audience. The baptismal font was made more visible. Simple meetinghouses really came into their own in the American colonies among various religious groups. The extremely plain houses used by rural Brethren and Friends, for example, even avoided any kind of raised pulpit (Fig. E). Frequently the seats were arranged so that the fellowship of the worshiping congregation was emphasized more than any altar, choir, or pulpit.

In recent years many of the so-called free or plain churches have moved away from their heritage, choosing either to imitate some Gothic or colonial pattern, or to build auditoriums that emphasize mass assembly rather than worship. Others have followed modern designs that seek to be functional as well as contemporary. Some recent developments encourage sanctuaries "in the round" or in some form that permits great flexibility in worship arrangements. While professional architects and builders can be helpful, the people who gather for worship should be considered in any design.

Fig. C

Fig. D

Fig. E

Buildings that encourage spiritual worship
With such a range of architectural patterns available, how can Christians choose the most appropriate environment for truly spiritual worship? Instead of offering specific guidelines, here are five questions for you to consider as you arrive at your own answers:

1. *Can a church building be authentic rather than imitative?* In other words, do Gothic arches mean anything for worshipers whose ideas and concepts are far from Gothic? Do we simply want to copy designs and patterns that seem "churchly," or can we find building materials and plans that really represent us?

2. *Can our church houses reflect the simplicity we value?* Not if they are planned to impress people by their ornaments and massive structures. Simple lines can provide the best design in the hands of an artist. But we may find it difficult to be satisfied with such plainness in our churches when our homes are no longer simple and plain.

3. *Can buildings serve people and not manipulate them?* Some church structures seem designed to force everyone into a mold. Others give you a sense of freedom and involvement in what is happening. Suppose you want to worship, not in rows, but face to face? Does the building permit or deny such expressions?

4. *Can buildings reflect your concern for service and mission?* If you went out to byways and side streets to invite people into your sanctuary, would the building welcome them, or would it say, "Be careful. Don't touch. I must be kept clean at all costs"? Can the structure encourage the ways you serve your community while serving your Lord?

5. *Can buildings offer flexibility and diversity?* Sometimes you need a sanctuary—almost literally—as a place of refuge from noise and confusion. Other times you want the visible and audible presence of all your friends. Does the solid concrete in your building set limits to enthusiastic activity or rule out new ways of worship? Must you renovate every ten years in order to keep up with the worship needs of your congregation?

12
Whatever Is Lovely:
Art in Worship

All that is true, all that is noble, all that is just and pure, all that is lovable and gracious, whatever is excellent and admirable—fill all your thoughts with these things. Phil. 4:8 (NEB)

Several years ago the *Gospel Messenger* featured on its cover an artist's portrayal of the Lord's Supper. The artist was Fritz Eichenberg, an illustrator whose etchings and woodcuts and designs for initials have appeared in editions of classics and in new publications. Attracted especially to the testimony of Quakers and also the work among the poor by certain Roman Catholic groups, Eichenberg often chose religious subjects for his art. His visual reconstruction of the Upper Room experience called for a round table sparsely furnished with food, surrounded by twelve men who could easily have walked in from a city street in their working clothes. The room itself was barren, devoid of ornaments, yet all the essential elements of Jesus' supper with his disciples were there, especially the relationship of twelve men to their Master.

The picture brought letters from readers. Some were offended because the artist's conception of Jesus and his disciples differed greatly from their own. Especially troublesome, for them, was the fact that the men in the picture seemed crude and ordinary, as if they had come in from Skid Row for a free meal and carried their dirt and filth with them. Others disliked the artist's portrayal of Jesus as being almost too human, too close to aspects of daily life they would prefer to forget. Still others missed the usual marks of "religious" art, the signs and symbols they associated with Christian devotion.

But other readers responded affirmatively. Not that the picture was beautiful, but it brought them closer to understanding the incarnation and to appreciating how even today Christ finds his home—and sometimes his warmest reception—among the poor and the homeless, among people who have little and who eagerly come to his table.

Have you ever listened in, when Christians vigorously debate the question of what constitutes great art? Most often the controversy rages over "modern" art, not because there is better understanding of traditional art, but because it has been around longer and seems less threatening. As we consider now the place of art and the environment it can help to create for worship, perhaps we can deal directly with some of the questions—and complaints—most often raised by persons who may not know much about art, but who definitely know what they like and dislike.

Questions we ask

1. *Why do so many religious artists deliberately distort and twist or exaggerate the subject they are picturing?* An artist will likely inform you that all art takes liberties with subject matter. If you want only an exact representation of a scene or of a person, then take a photograph. The artist offers something quite different by what seems to be distortion or exaggeration. The artist can help you use your eyes in a new way, catching the shapes or colors that convey feelings about a subject. For example, in Albrecht Durer's famous study of hands, he could have tried merely to copy hands folded or touched

together. But instead he distorted the reality by making the hands narrow, the fingers long, and positioning them so that they suggest a soaring Gothic arch. They are not, therefore, pictured hands, but "praying" hands, and they have become almost a universal symbol for prayer. The artist takes liberties with nature for a purpose that is not merely wilful. Often the artist helps us find within nature or beyond nature some insight or truth or feeling we cannot see alone.

2. *Why do artists take such liberties with history in dealing with biblical or religious subjects?* If artists set out to illustrate a Bible dictionary or a book of history, we would expect them to offer an accurate and reliable picture of what is known about a particular time and place. But usually that is not their purpose. So throughout the years artists have tended to portray biblical scenes and events in the context of the world the artist knows firsthand. In the work of an Italian artist the Mary in a nativity scene will not be Jewish, but Italian. Oriental artists can be expected to conceive of New Testament characters as oriental. Indeed hardly any of the classic artists we take for granted when we think of religious art have tried to picture Palestine as it was and is, or Bible persons as they might have appeared. What this says is not that artists are lazy or careless, but, rather, that they tend to see the universal and timeless characteristics of their subjects. In so doing they can help worshipers identify what is eternally contemporary in our Christian faith.

3. *Why do I find it so hard to understand what an artist is saying?* Perhaps because you want an immediate explanation about something not easily explained. Or it may be that the artist is not nearly as interested in "saying" something as in "sharing" something. Think of the artist's creation the same way you think of a gift offered to you by a friend. In accepting the gift you help in the communication process. It's like accepting a handclasp or a friendly hug. You may think about the gift you receive for years, and what it says to you is a combination of what it pictures in itself and what it reveals about

the person who gave it. So it is with a work of art offered to God and to other human beings. Perhaps the artist will be happy to point out some obvious "message,"
but allow the art itself to speak to you. It can even
"mean" something to you that never occured to the artist.

Art in the service of the church
In its various forms, from early Hebrew times until our
own, the worship of God has enlisted the creative talents
of artists. Consider, for example, the recognition in Exodus (35:30—39:43) that certain artists, Bezalel of the
tribe of Audah and Oholiab of the tribe of Dan, were
filled both "with the Spirit of God" and "with ability . . .
to devise artistic designs." Therefore, in a unique way
they could assist in making the tabernacle of God a
beautiful place. Using the gifts of the people, they could
design its furnishing and create vestments and equipment
for the use of priests. The story is offered in great detail
as an explanation of the worship environment provided
for the people of Israel.

Yet the Hebrews, while appreciating the service of
art, also were explicitly commanded not to make any
graven images, either of God or of many aspects of his
creation (Read Deut. 4:15-31). In one way this may seem
to be an extreme prohibition, since it meant that some
aspects of pictorial art were denied to the Hebrew people. Still it reflected a profound insight that artistic
creations can become idols, can become objects of
worship instead of aids to worship.

Perhaps if we keep in mind both the values and the
dangers, we can understand why in the history of the
Christian church there have been times when art has
been used in great elaboration for liturgical purposes
while in other periods art has been rejected amost completely as contributing to idolatry. We need also to
remember that in times when most worshipers were il-
literate, the use of familiar symbols, the representation of
biblical scenes and characters in stone and glass, and the
creation of furnishings for the church were often means

for informing worshipers as well as assisting them in their worship.

Though Christians share with Jews an abhorrence for idols and a strong sense of awe in the presence of the invisible God, we also believe that in Jesus Christ the word became flesh, that Christ is the image of the invisible God (Col. 1:15-20), that he lived among us, and his presence continues in his church. So it is not surprising that, within limits at least, the Christian church has not excluded either painting or sculpture, and art has been put to work to serve the needs of the church. The church has employed artists, has been a patron of the arts, and today encourages the contribution that art can make to worship. Here let us note just briefly some of the art forms that have enriched the life of the church.

1. *Icons.* Every visitor to an Eastern Orthodox church notices at once the iconostasis, a wall covered with icons that separates the nave from the sanctuary. Icons are different from paintings by individual artists in that they are two-dimensional religious pictures which Orthodox believers regard as "transparent windows through which the faithful can see beyond." They are painted by anonymous artists following ancient instructions. The icon is to be venerated but not worshiped. It offers to the worshiper a visual reminder of the history of salvation.

2. *Mosaics.* Early Christian churches in Southern Europe had few windows but large wall spaces. These provided a place for artists to use glassy stones, sometimes covered with gold leaf, called mosaics, not only in patterns but also in vivid pictures that seem to shine with a mysterious glory. They are most effective when seen at a distance. Some of the best examples of Christian art in mosaics can be seen in Italy (at Ravenna and Venice) and in Byzantine churches in Greece and Turkey.

3. *Frescoes.* Another early form of Christian art was less costly than working with mosaics but more flexible and naturalistic. These paintings are called frescoes because a painter will mix his colors with a thin coating of plaster that is still wet. Frescoes resemble water colors

more than oil paintings. Frescoes can be found in catacomb paintings, in the vast decorations that Giotto painted in the Arena Chapel in Padua, and in the master-pieces that Michelangelo produced in the Sistine Chapel in Rome—to name only a few illustrations of this widely used art form.

4. *Illuminated manuscripts.* Before the invention of printing from movable type, Bibles and prayerbooks were laboriously copied by hand, often in monasteries, by trained scribes. They decorated their pages not with specific illustrations so much as by elaborate initials and even small paintings that could brighten or "illuminate" the text. The scribes used various colors as well as gold and silver.

5. *Sculpture and woodcarvings.* Congregations that had no access to books during the Middle Ages (books were limited and in a strange language) depended often on sculptured figures and wood carvings in their cathedrals and parish churches for much of their religious instruction. Though often a poor substitute for verbal or written lessons, these portrayals of biblical scenes and events from church history offered one way in which certain works of art might be said to serve as "the poor man's Bible." The cathedral of Chartres, in France, is said to contain ten thousand painted or sculptured human figures.

6. *Paintings.* New opportunities for artists came with the discovery of oil painting in the 15th century. Slow to dry, oil painting allowed the artist to add one layer to another and to achieve new effects. Many of the treasures of Christian art in the Renaissance and modern periods came to us through the use of this medium.

Art as interpretation—the face of Christ
If Jesus Christ was and is "the image of the invisible God," if indeed "in him all the fulness of God was pleased to dwell," as Paul affirms, we cannot help being curious about the appearance of Jesus, how he looked to the persons among whom he lived in a particular period of human history. Putting aside some unlikely

traditions—that a veil or a robe captured some indications of his appearance—we are resigned to the fact that no one really knows how Jesus looked. Even the verbal descriptions we have from eyewitnesses have something far more important to tell us than the physical details about which we are curious.

Undoubtedly artists in various ages have helped to form our mental images of Jesus, but at best they have told us more about themselves and their times than they have indicated about his appearance. Yet each one in some measure may also have helped us discover some facet of Jesus' personality we may have previously ignored. It is worthwhile, therefore, to examine some of the different interpretations that artists suggest regarding the face of Christ.

1. *The Byzantine Christ.* Step into an ancient church and let your eyes turn upward to the mosaics that adorn the central dome or the concave area over the altar. Most prominent and striking will be the figure of Christ, whose eyes look directly down upon you. Perhaps the best example of such a Christ figure can be found in the cathedral at Cefalu, in Sicily. Here is Christ as ruler and judge. He is an awesome monarch already positioned so that he can be surrounded by a heavenly court of angels and saints.

2. *Giotto.* To move from a Byzantine mozaic to the frescoes of Giotto, often called the first modern painter though he lived in the 14th century, is to observe how a painter views Christ in the light of human relationship. Giotto filled the walls of the Arena Chapel in Padua, Italy, with a series of frescoes reviewing the life of Mary and the life of Jesus. One can still see a nimbus, or halo, around the head of Christ. But there are more natural characteristics indicated as Jesus washes his disciples' feet, eats with them in the Upper Room, and faces trial and crucifixion.

3. *Leonardo.* Far more familiar is Leonardo DaVinci's painting of *The Last Supper,* filled with fascinating character studies of the disciples and focused on the moment when Jesus announces that one of them will betray

him. One of Leonardo's contemporaries observed that the artist was never satisfied with his portrayal of the face of Christ and that in one sense it was never really completed. Despite the damage that has been done to the painting since Leonardo's time, it remains one of the most beloved examples of Christian art.

4. *El Greco.* A 16th-century artist, born in Crete and apprenticed in Italy, found his spiritual home in Spain where he was simply known as El Greco, "the Greek." His religious paintings, many of which can be seen in museums around the world as well as in Spain, communicate a feeling about a spiritual world that transcends even when it permeates the material world. His paintings that deal with the life of Christ show us elongated figures that seem almost distorted, but the effect is always to underline some inner quality—as in his painting of the resurrection in which the upward moving lines accentuate the triumph of Christ over death.

5. *Rembrandt.* Few artists have been more conversant with the Bible than Rembrandt (145 paintings, 70 etchings and 575 drawings of biblical subjects). As he grew in understanding through his study, he moved away from painting Christ in glory and began to represent him as more human. He painted many pictures in which the face of Christ, still so marked by humanity, seems to be surrounded by rays of light, not a halo but a suggestion that Christ was also more than human.

6. *Holman Hunt.* One of the best known portraits of Christ is the work of a British artist who was influenced by two important movements in 19th century England: the pre-Raphaelite group of artists, of which Holman Hunt was a member; and the Oxford Movement, which looked for traditional values in the Church of England and which revived interest in its medieval heritage. Hunt's painting is called *The Light of the World* and depicts Christ as bearing a lantern and knocking on the door of the human heart. It pictures a loving but slightly remote Christ whose head is surrounded by light even though his features seem human. The painting incorporates many biblical symbols and directly illustrates a

text, Rev. 3:20. The picture is most effective in its original color and can be viewed at the chapel of Keble College in Oxford and in St. Paul's Cathedral in London.

7. *Rouault.* Georges Rouault, a French artist who died in 1958, was a devout Christian who created many portraits of Christ, some in a series of black and white prints in the 1920's and others in stained glass. Some are in paintings that use bold lines and heavy colors to emphasize the passion of a Christ who out of pity and love for human beings accepted mockery and pain and death. Several of his images of Christ seem to echo the servant poems of Isaiah (Isa. 53 especially) that look forward to the "suffering servant" who gave his life on the cross.

8. *Contemporary images.* Just as artists from different periods of Christian history have offered strikingly different concepts of Christ (usually in surroundings that reflect their own time), so do artists today around the world bring us images of Christ that may take us by surprise (a black Christ, a Christ with oriental or Latin features) because we so easily forget that our own conceptions of him (as white, Anglo-Saxon, certainly not as a first-century Hebrew) are determined by our own limited vision.

Art as environment for worship

The building in which we worship, especially the place of meeting we usually think of as a "sanctuary" is an important factor in determining an environment for worship. But in addition to those rather permanent aspects of church architecture we discuss in another chapter, there are varied ways in which, from Sunday to Sunday, or from one time of meeting to another, we can employ the artistic creativity of members in our faith family to enliven and illumine the surroundings of even the simplest place of worship.

Listen to an artist's comment on environment. Joyce Miller says, "We have worked hard in the past to use words and music to tell the Christian story, but we have neglected the effect of color and design as a worship aid. . . . We are all affected by color, and design. We identify specific movements of line and specific colors with certain emotions. The arrangement of furniture and objects in a worship setting can create feelings either of boredom or of excitement."

Listen to a pastor's observation. Jack Lowe says, "If God had been as uncreative in creating the world as we are in creating our worship environment, most of us would not want to live in the world. Yet a reading of Genesis 1 and 2 reminds us that God's creativity has given us variety in our living—day and night; sun, moon and stars; seasons; flowers and trees; fish, birds, and mammals; male and female. For people who seek to be Godlike, we have forgotten one of God's characteristics—creativity."

Consider a few of the ways in which we can control the environment of worship. The *furnishings* of our places for meeting may be somewhat permanent, but hopefully they can also be modified or changed. A church that values simplicity should examine its furnishings to see if they are plain rather than ornate, if they are adapted to the needs of the congregation or if they are merely "extras," if they are flexible and movable rather than permanent, if they convey a sense of naturalness rather than of artificiality.

In recent years *banners,* often designed by individuals or groups in a congregation, have helped not only to create an atmosphere for worship but also to interpret ideas and themes by way of pictures and symbols. The psalmist wrote, "In the name of God set up our banners!" (Psalm 20:5). Sometimes the banners of old contained warlike threats and affirmations, and they seemed to belong to the pageantry of royal processions. They may still serve such purposes, on occasions in church, but they also may serve a less dramatic role. Their messages can underline the theme of a service or a special occasion. They offer a means for sharing insights that are meaningful for the persons who create them and for other members of the community. The simplest church can be brightened and enlivened by handcrafted banners.

The *bulletins* we use in our services can facilitate many aspects of a congregation's worship, providing an outline of the order of worship, indicating readings or songs calling for participation by everyone present, caring for announcements and information important to the church family. Frequently they offer scripture texts with interpretive comments and sometimes new worship aids are printed and shared in this way. But bulletins may also utilize photography and art to illustrate a theme. Many of the bulletin series we use are based on the lectionary used by many denominations and follow the sequence of readings suggested for the Christian year. Others are designed for special local or denominational observances. Perhaps the most creative bulletins, however, are those that are designed and made (perhaps by silk-screening) by members of the congregation.

Not as common in plain or "free" churches as in liturgical churches are *vestments,* the robes or special garments worn by pastors or choir members. In one sense a robe sets a minister apart from the congregation, a distinction some try to avoid. Yet some pastors and choir leaders actually choose robes because they feel less conspicuous than in ordinary street dress, and they feel that this uniformity of dress actually contributes to a worship atmosphere. Others believe that the diversity of dress within a congregation adds to the color and joy that should accompany worship.

Few persons would be inclined to complain about the contribution that *flowers* and *plants* make to a worship setting, especially if they are used in natural ways that recall the outdoors with all its reminders of God's continuing creativity in providing a world of beauty as our dwelling place. *Candles* provide warmth and a feeling of homelikeness in many settings as well as useful symbolism and a contribution to a worshipful atmosphere.

Many of these elements are regularly combined into *visual centers* in our places of meeting, which we have traditionally called "worship centers." That term is misleading, especially when we think of worship as an expression of meeting—with one another and with our Lord. In one sense, if there is any center of worship, it should be the presence of God in our midst—and there is danger in trying to localize that presence. But there is still need for certain visual centers as a part of worship environment. Perhaps we would be helped in our worship if these were not always at the same location—on an "altar" or "communion table" for every occasion. Changing the visual center from time to time might help us discover new insights into the ways God's presence is made evident in and to a worshiping congregation.

Art as an offering to God

There are works of art that have no religious subject matter and serve no specific function for an activity of the church. Yet they may have been created as an act of devotion and offered to the Christian community simply as a gift of beauty to be shared. For such creations—a painting, perhaps; a sculpture; a woodcarving; a poster or banner—there ought to be a time and a place for the church family to exhibit them appropriately and to demonstrate a happy "acceptance" of an artist's creation. Unfortunately some artists have been rebuffed when they sincerely wanted to share their joy in creation—simply because other Christians had different tastes and seemed unable to appreciate the fact that a gift was offered. Despite our differences in taste and understanding regarding art, we need to become more sensitive to the genuineness of every artist's offering and by our openness we may help such talents to be dedicated—as all our talents should be—to the glory of God.

13
New Ways in Worship: What Hope for Renewal?

"Behold! I am making all things new!" Rev. 21:5 (NEB)

New forms of worship? The members of First Church can talk about them now without rising blood pressure, but everyone remembers a Sunday several years ago when the "new forms" arrived with a bang—literally. It was Youth Sunday, always a time to recognize youth, yet seldom to involve them in planning worship. On this occasion the youth were encouraged to take full responsibility for the service—and some of them grasped at a once-for-all chance to introduce new ideas.

In retrospect, most of their innovations don't seem so revolutionary, but at that time the congregation was hardly prepared for electric guitars with loud amplification or music that pounded the walls and set a steady beat. Now the songs are familiar, but then few of the older members could figure out why "Born Free" or "The Sounds of Silence" or "We Shall Overcome" belonged in church. They listened to—and liked—the message of "They'll Know We Are Christians by Our Love," but the handclapping that accompanied it was new for First Church.

Instead of reading a call to worship, the young leader

simply said, "Good morning." Her scripture readings—in a paraphrase from the "Cotton Patch" version of the New Testament—sounded a little like the Bible, but the setting seemed to be in the United States. And the morning prayer troubled some listeners because the young participant was asking, "Are you running with me, Jesus?"

Other innovations included the showing of slides depicting the struggles of migrant workers, a recording of a rock number by the Beatles, and an interpretation of the Lord's Prayer in symbolic movement—which some thought was tastefully done and others regarded as "dancing in church." There were bright colored banners on the walls, and a spotlight was focused on a vivid poster. At the conclusion the young people, all of them, moved out into the congregation with their hands extended for a greeting and friendly blessing.

The reactions were mixed. Many adults were enthusiastic about the eager participation of youth even if some features were not to their taste. The change from services was so great, however, that many longtime members were upset. No one walked out, but a few warned the pastor that this was going too far—such antics might be appropriate elsewhere, they thought, but not in the Lord's house. Some frankly were confused. The content of the service seemed to be legitimate, but the poetry and music and graphics seemed out of place. And the music—some called it noise—was far too loud. It was obvious that no one fell asleep and that something happened, but just what happened and whether it was worship was a question for debate for several weeks.

Is it worship renewal—or the enjoyment of novelty?
Today most congregations have been exposed to new, different, often experimental forms of worship. The novelty and the shock has worn off, to the extent that new ways of singing praise to God, new touches of color and design in the church sanctuary, and some new rituals of celebrating the faith have been widely accepted. There is a flood of resource books that offer new liturgies, new

songs, new treatments of traditional observances—as well as stimulating books making the case for celebrative events worthy of a new freedom in worship.

For many, mostly younger members, the changes meet an urgent need. The language and patterns familiar to an earlier generation often fail to speak in any meaningful way of God's present activity in this world. Worshipers may feel that they cannot go through motions and repeat phrases that are empty and dead. If singing a new song to the Lord, if translating the gospel message into today's language, if stepping up the tempo of celebration can renew a sense of spiritual dynamic in the congregation, then by all means let us welcome the contribution of new worship patterns. In doing so we need not reject what continues to be of meaning and worth in older traditions. Indeed we may rediscover some of the treasures of the past, finding that they speak to our present needs.

The important consideration is that we not be carried away by every novelty that someone can think of or be led astray by new winds of doctrine. The "in" thing for the moment can be hopelessly out of date by next year. Instead, we ought to examine carefully and openly some of the movements that promise renewal in worship. No single development may meet our expectations, but we can appropriate the values that commend themselves to our congregational needs. Let us take a brief look at several such forces at work in Christian congregations today, including the Church of the Brethren.

Many forces at work

1. *Charismatic renewal.* A dynamic force among Christians today, one that cuts across denominational and organizational lines, is a kind of pentecostalism that emphasizes gifts of the Spirit. Catholic and Protestant church members from various traditions have joined in worship expressions that are surprisingly free and spontaneous. The word "charismatic," referring specifically to the spiritual gifts Paul discusses in 1 Cor. 12, has been appropriated by these movements even though only a

few of the New Testament gifts of the Spirit are emphasized by their adherents.

The charismatic influence on contemporary worship may turn out to be profound. For reasons we have often noted in these pages many church members have found their services dull or static, far too rigid or impersonal for their taste. Seeking release, they have discovered a new liberty and a contagious enthusiasm in gatherings that take their model—and their generating force—from the day of Pentecost. Charismatic worship is often marked by speaking and singing in tongues, by services of healing, and by testimonies to receiving the baptism of the Holy Spirit.

Charismatic worship tends to be joyful and loud, with little self-consciousness or worry about appearances. Obviously its expressions will vary with the background of the participants; and in some cases, as in Corinth in New Testament times, it may lead to excesses. While its positive values clearly offer a revitalizing force, charismatics and noncharismatics alike must be alert to the problem that Paul observed among the Corinthians. The early church, in the initial glow of Christ's resurrection and in the power of Pentecost, had found a new freedom in celebrating their life in Christ. But, without restraint, the exercise of individualism threatened to destroy the church community. Some gifts were valued far above others. Some marks of the Spirit became objects of unspiritual pride. Some members forgot they were members of a body—and not its head. So Paul· sought to restore a sense of proportion and a degree of order by reminding them of the supremacy of Christ and of "the more excellent way" of love. Above all they were to yield to one another, discerning the body of believers and its needs, and to use their charismatic gifts modestly, intelligently, lovingly, for the good of all.

Christian worship today should be enriched by *all* the gifts that people bring—those which Paul enumerated and others which are as varied as humans are—to the service and praise of God. But worship must also give evidence of the fruits of the Spirit—if true renewal is to come.

2. *Liturgical renewal.* Though many Christians tend to look askance at liturgy, as if it contained only formal, unchanging readings and rituals, the word itself, as we have already noted, refers to the service or work that lay persons as well as clergy perform in a ministry of worship. In recent years, among the churches that have stayed close to a formal liturgy there have been efforts to rediscover the values of liturgical worship and to experiment with new liturgies that will help to relate the eternal gospel to modern life. Among Roman Catholics the most notable changes have been the use of English in place of Latin in many services and the placement of altars so that the priest celebrating mass is facing the congregation. Increasingly lay members are given more responsibility for leadership. In the Anglican communion the process of prayer book revision is under way in the Church of England and the Episcopal Church in the United States. Eastern Orthodox leaders have also been searching for ways "to recover authenticity in worship and thereby authenticity of faith." Several Lutheran groups, for the sake of unity as well as worship renewal, have encouraged liturgical reforms.

Renewal efforts have led to a greater diversity of worship forms in churches that were not formerly accustomed to many changes. The new proposals are welcomed by some, but resisted by others who prefer the ceremonies and the language they learned in childhood.

3. *Ecumenical activities.* Many Christians who have been active in the ecumenical movement both in this country and overseas have looked for worship enrichment to follow from increasing interchurch activity. Indeed in ecumenical gatherings, participants can expect to be bound together more closely by worship services that celebrate the unity that Christians feel. Through ecumenical studies, publications, and activities all over the world, Christians discover how Christ is understood and how God is worshiped in various traditions and customs, in languages and symbols that may be sharply different and yet equally valid.

Yet there are disappointments too. As Christians

from different traditions are drawn together they find greater frustration in some of the barriers that still separate them—especially when they are prevented from freely and openly sharing in the eucharist around one common table. Another disappointment lies in the difficulty of manifesting the same spirit of unity in one's own local community that one can experience in an ecumenical conference. Despite the fears of persons loyal to their own traditions, ecumenical participation need not lose sight of what is unique in each of our churches. Rather, the ecumenical setting may help us appreciate that we have something original to share with others. Yet such fears persist.

4. *Renewal and retreat centers.* In a study that Olive Wyon made a few years ago of renewal movements within the church in Europe, the British theologian and writer compared them to "living springs" of water that bubble up out of dry ground and promise new life to thirsty persons. If she were to make a similar study today of dozens of retreat centers and renewal movements within the United States as well as in Europe or elsewhere in the world, she would need several volumes to describe how such developments—some sponsored by churches, some by individuals, some by interchurch groups—provide refreshment and restoration to thousands of Christians. The new life they find "in retreat" or in conference or in common service is shared in many ways throughout the life of all our churches.

In most instances worship experiences in retreat settings seem to have a reviving effect on us, clarifying our vision and strengthening our commitment. The trouble is that we find it difficult to sustain the "mountaintop" character of such experiences in the day-by-day and week-after-week environment where we live out our lives. And worship, we must say again, to be effective must work its transformation at home, in the local congregation, if it is to be vital and meaningful for everyone.

5. *The contribution of the arts.* The close interrelationship between Christian worship and the arts has already been mentioned and illustrated in earlier

chapters. Here we want simply to observe that the enthusiastic welcome that many churches and church leaders now offer to artists, musicians, craftspersons, and others with creative talents has been mutually beneficial. Artists have often felt estranged from the church, but the opportunity to share their gifts and to see how their contributions in art serve as aids to worship has given them a new interest in various phases of the church's program. And—let's be frank about it—though we sometimes complain about all the newfangled things that are coming into the church, many of us take real delight in the creative touches of the artist's imagination that add interest and variety to what we do Sunday after Sunday.

The danger is that we become so fascinated by the art that we forget the purpose of our coming together. Or we lose ourselves in the beauty of a service, allowing it to lull us to sleep, neglecting the sharp prophetic voices that should stir us to action. And artsy-craftsy people sometimes seem to suggest that only those who are "creative" in obvious ways are really serving the Lord. This is not the intention of genuine artists, of course. The ones who are most desirous of serving the church are eager to see that each member's gifts are recognized and offered to God. This is the contribution in the arts we should welcome—a sense of the creative in every worshiper.

6. *The rediscovery of bodily movement.* Most persons think of worship as a kind of passive activity that takes place while you are seated in a pew. Of course there are times for standing, perhaps also for kneeling. But generally we think of worship as something rather static for which we remain in one place for an hour. This may be due to our Puritan heritage of strict Sunday observances and prohibitions against too much activity. Or it may also result from the tendency during the Middle Ages to shift responsibility in worship from people to priest. In any case, such a passive attitude, we now believe, is not adequate for real participation.

One place for bodily movement in worship is evident in religious drama. Dramatic episodes, sometimes centered on familiar Bible stories, at other times based on a contemporary problem, serve not merely as something to watch but as legitimate expressions of worship. The familiar rituals associated with baptism and the love feast or even such regular activities as receiving an offering and presenting it in some graphic way—all of these exercises in movement are part of the drama of worship. Drama need not be staged behind a curtain or before footlights. Drama has a natural place in the chancel or elsewhere in a church sanctuary as a central ingredient in worship.

When you mention the prospect of dancing as related to worship, many persons are troubled by their feelings about some kinds of social dancing or dancing that is primarily for exhibition or entertainment. We tend to overlook the observation in Eccles. 3:4 that there is "a time to dance" as well as a time to mourn, or the call to Hebrew worshipers in Psalm 150 to praise God "with timbrel and dance." Jesus himself urged his followers, when persecuted, to "rejoice in that day and leap for joy" (Luke 6:23). These and other references to bodily expressions of joyful worship may not convince you that Jesus can best be described as "Lord of the Dance," to quote a recent song; but at least they remind us that it was not unusual either for Hebrew or Christian worshipers to express their profound emotions in activity similar to dancing.

We sing carols at Christmas, often unaware that carols were originally circle dances and that some of the terms we associate with sacred music, such as "stanza" and "chorus" came from instructions for movement. Many of our traditions associated with camp meetings and assemblies also involved marching, singing, and dancing together. And in summer camps and conferences recent generations have discovered that many folk songs and games have a religious origin and contribute to worship as well as to recreation.

But even apart from drama and dance, movement has been and continues to be essential to worship. Charismatic services emphasize the words of 1 Tim. 2:3

"pray, lifting holy hands." Eastern Orthodox worshipers will often prostrate themselves, falling flat on the floor, as a gesture of confession. Many groups encourage kneeling as an important bodily preparation for prayer. Brethren have traditionally thought that the salutation or holy kiss, accompanied by a handshake, should be observed either as a ritual act in the love feast or as a greeting when brother meets brother and sister meets sister. In some traditions the salutation is threefold, in honor of the Trinity. A similar gesture is "passing the peace" from hand to hand with a spoken blessing.

Many congregations now celebrate some special event such as the reception of new members or the dedication of babies by forming a "circle of love" around the persons for whom they ask special blessings. The touching of hand to hand, a physical act, reinforces and validates the words that are spoken. In a similar way the physical act of literally washing another's feet illustrates better than any words what it means to serve and to be cleansed. Though there is a need to guard against excesses in physical activity, no one can question the need for worship words to be translated into worship gestures. For worship can never be passive. It must also lead to action—and mostly that involves some kind of bodily movement.

What Brethren can contribute to worship renewal
If Church of the Brethren congregations will examine their own heritage in worship and make a conscious effort to adopt and interpret its values for contemporary use, they will not only enrich their own services but they may also have some specific practices to share with the larger Christian community. For instance:

1. The Brethren love feast is far more than a standard observance to be followed on communion Sundays. It is a scripturally based drama calling for a full measure of participation by all members. It follows closely the pattern of the Upper Room, but it is also close to the common life of people today. It has movement and drama, uses everyday symbols, is indeed a happening

among those present. But most of all the love feast is a witness to God's ongoing offering of love through Jesus Christ. It provides many options for creativity in following a traditional pattern. It promises to have increasing significance for Christians who not only look back to the Bible, or who look within themselves around the table, but who also look beyond for opportunities for loving service.

2. The Brethren healing service is also scripturally based in the practice of anointing. It offers a ritual that applies to personal and family needs as well as having meaning for the church. It avoids many of the pitfalls that accompany publicly-staged healing services. It relates to contemporary interests and offers needed worship values.

3. Group singing among Brethren, notably at conferences but not only there, contains great promise for encouraging more direct lay involvement in times of praise and thanksgiving. Other musical resources can supplement and enrich a tradition honored by Brethren. Hearty singing meets many of the basic needs for a congregation to discover and express itself as a living expression of the body of Christ.

4. Lay participation and lay leadership in worship grow naturally out of the Brethren tradition of ministry and service. Creativity can be applied now to ways of underlining the responsibility for every member—not only clergy or designated leaders—to "lead" in worship.

5. Worship and work belong together. Each is a service rendered to God on behalf of human beings. At a time when many are dissatisfied with verbalizing their faith, Brethren have an opportunity to demonstrate the intimate relationship between words and deeds, between worship and mission, between holiness and wholeness, as an expression of what it means to be a Christian.

Come, let us worship—in spirit and in truth.

For Study and Action

Chapter 1

1. Take time to read carefully the Bible passages referred to, noting especially any characteristics of worship they illustrate: Deut. 26:1-11; Psalm 8; Isa. 6:1-8; John 4:19-24; Rom. 12:1; 1 John 4:11; and Rev. 4:9-11.

2. Without trying to be precise or comprehensive, write one or two sentences indicating what worship means to you.

3. Find your church directory or listing of members. Then take any worship bulletin for a recent Sunday. List the names of five persons for whom you think the recent service was well suited. List the names of five others who may have been indifferent or turned off. Was your own name on either list? Can you recall any service that you think was meaningful for at least 80 percent of those in attendance?

4. Glance through the pages of this study book, noting what each chapter is about. On the table of contents page use a pencil to mark an "x" beside the topic that now interests you most. Put a check mark beside the subject you know least about. (After completing your reading and study, you can decide if you would mark them in the same way.)

Hardin, H. Grady; Quillian, Joseph D.; and White, James F. *The Celebration of the Gospel.* Nashville: Abingdon, 1964, 192 pages (especially chapter 1).

Randolph, David James. *God's Party, A Guide to New Forms of Worship.* Nashville: Abingdon, 1975, 144 pages (especially chapter 1).

Skoglund, John E. *Worship in the Free Churches.* Valley Forge: The Judson Press, 1965, 156 pages (especially chapters 1 and 3).

White, James F. *New Forms of Worship.* New York: Abingdon, 1971, 222 pages (especially chapters 1 and 2).

Chapter 2

1. Make your own evaluation of what you consider to be the strengths and weaknesses or worship in the Hebrew temple. On the plus side note the various positive characteristics of individual and group worship that are suggested in Psalm 24 and Isaiah 6:1-8. Perhaps you can think of other values that impress you in the setting of the central temple and its various ceremonies, including antiphonal singing and impressive

pageantry. Over against these values list the problems that you are aware of, including the harsh judgments passed by prophets like Jeremiah, Amos, and Micah, as well as some of the problems related to temple worship that were apparent in the time of Jesus.

2. Try to recall worship experiences you have had in settings that may be somewhat similar to a temple, such as a convocation at a university chapel, a major service at an Annual Conference, or perhaps a service that you attended in a Roman Catholic church or some other that involved more ceremonies and more liturgy than you are accustomed to.

3. Select three hymns from your hymnal that are based upon psalms. Place the words of the hymn text side by side with the psalm as it appears in poetic form in one of the more recent translations. You may want to compare Psalm 100 with the hymn "All People That on Earth Do Dwell"; Psalm 30 with "O God, Our Help in Ages Past"; Psalm 46 with "A Mighty Fortress Is Our God"; or Psalm 23 with "The King of Love My Shepherd Is."

Davies, Horton. *Christian Worship—Its History and Meaning.* New York: Abingdon Press, 1957, 128 pages (especially chapter 1).

Hedley, George. *When Protestants Worship.* New York: Abingdon, 1961, 96 pages.

Jones, Ilion T. *A Historical Approach to Evangelical Worship.* New York: Abingdon Press, 1954, 319 pages (especially Part I, Chapter 1).

Scammon, John H. *Living With the Psalms.* Valley Forge: Judson Press, 1967, 157 pages.

Simpson, William W. *Jewish Prayer and Worship.* Naperville: S.C.M. Book Club, 1965, 128 pages (especially Part I).

Chapter 3

1. Take a local church worship outline—from your own church or another—and select the activities that resemble New Testament worship practices.

2. Examine a hymnal in order to determine to what extent the contents include "psalms" (look in the index of text sources for those directly based on the Psalms), "hymns, and spiritual songs" (would this include Negro spirituals and gospel songs?).

3. For your own devotional use make a brief anthology of New Testament prayers (include the Lord's Prayer, the prayer

of the Jerusalem church in Acts 4, others you find in Paul's letters); hymns (choose one of the nativity hymns in Luke, one from Paul's letters like 1 Cor. 13, one from Rev. 4, 5, or 19); and benedictions (there are several in the Epistles). A modern translation of the New Testament will help you locate passages of poetry.

4. Try to imagine what would happen if Jesus were to participate in your Sunday service. What rituals would he accept and follow? At what points might he encounter opposition?

5. Only a few churches now observe the Lord's Supper or communion service every Sunday. Would you like to see some parts of it included in regular Sunday services? Do occasional church dinners preserve the value of the New Testament "love feast" Would you favor Brethren observances more frequently?

6. Can freedom for individual expression (in testimonies, "sharing" times, speaking in tongues, spontaneous singing or shouting) be carried too far in today's worship services as it was in Corinth? How do you view this "danger" in contrast with the "danger" of a strictly ordered service?

Davies, Horton. *Christian Worship—Its History and Meaning.* New York: Abingdon, 1957, 128 pages (especially chapter 2).

Hahn, Ferdinand. *The Worship of the Early Church.* Philadelphia: Fortress Press, 1973, 118 pages.

Hedley, George. *When Protestants Worship.* New York: Abingdon, 1961, 96 pages (especially chapter 3).

Jones, Ilion T. *A Historical Approach to Evangelical Worship.* New York: Abingdon Press, 1954, 319 pages (especially Part I, chapters 2 and 3).

Martin, Ralph P. *Worship in the Early Church.* Grand Rapids: Eerdmans, 1975, 144 pages (especially chapters 2 and 3).

Snyder, Graydon. "A Day With Fortunatus," *Messenger.* November 23, 1967.

Chapter 4

1. For your Bible study examine passages of scripture that call attention to prominent characteristics of worship convictions, such as Mark 16:1-6 (Eastern Orthodox); 1 Cor. 11:23-26 (Roman Catholic); Rom. 5:1-5 (Lutheran); Psalm 34:1-3 (Anglican); Psalm 100 and Psalm 124:8 (Reformed); 2 Cor. 3:17-18 (Free churches); John 1:9-13 (Quaker).

2. Look in a Friday or Saturday edition of your local

newspaper at the announcements or listings of church services. How do they reflect the different worship traditions mentioned in this chapter? Recall any churches you have visited, and decide how you would describe the service: liturgical, informal, casual, or perhaps so free that nothing is prearranged.

3. If you were serving on a committee to plan an ecumenical service of worship for your community, what elements from the various traditions would you like to include? At what points would it be possible for Roman Catholics and Protestants to worship together?

4. Make a note of any worship tradition you have studied or heard about that runs counter to some basic conviction of yours. Can you defend your position? How do you feel about reciting a creed, crossing yourself, lighting a candle before a picture or statue, singing in Latin or Greek, taking communion from a common cup, standing for long periods of time, kneeling before you enter a pew, clapping your hands in rhythm to a song, lifting up both hands in praise to God, chanting responses, or joining in a procession?

Bainton, Roland H. *Here I Stand, a Life of Martin Luther.* New York: Abingdon-Cokesbury, 1950, 422 pages.

Barkley, John M. *The Worship of the Reformed Church.* Richmond: John Knox Press, 1967, 132 pages (especially chapters I, II, III, and XIII).

Benz, Ernst. *The Eastern Orthodox Church.* New York: Doubleday & Co., 1963, 230 pages.

Davies, Horton. *Christian Worship—Its History and Meaning.* New York: Abingdon Press, 1957, 128 pages (especially chapters 3-8).

Hedley, George. *When Protestants Worship.* New York: Abingdon, 1961, 96 pages (especially chapter 4).

Jones, Ilion T. *A Historical Approach to Evangelical Worship. New York: Abingdon Press, 1954, 319 pages (especially Part I, chapters 4, 5 and 6).*

Chapter 5

1. Read again some of the familiar Bible passages you have listened to during the observance of Brethren ordinances (John 13:1-17; 1 Cor. 11:23-29; Matt. 28:19-20; Rom. 6:1-4; James 5:14-16).

2. Many worship practices emphasized by Brethren result

from a literal following of Bible passages. Make your own assessment of the values and dangers of such literalism. Reflect on your own feelings regarding services you may have attended as a child or teenager. Was the emphasis on obedience over-done? Did the symbolic arrangements and actions encourage you to think more about what being a Christian should mean to you?

3. Some recent innovations in observing the love feast have departed from literalism but have attempted to relate the basic service to more contemporary concerns, as by cleaning shoes in place of feetwashing, or identifying the Lord's Supper with a potluck meal. Does this "modernizing" help or hinder your participation in the service?

4. The early church observed love feast and communion, we think, much as Brethren understand it. But they also held their agape meals much more frequently, perhaps every Sunday. Could the communion service be held more often without losing some values of a major event once or twice a year?

5. Try to recall the most recent love feast you attended. What rituals—either the traditional rites or the customs that go along with them—impressed you most? How could the service be enriched?

Beahm, William M. *The Brethren Love Feast.* Elgin: The Brethren Press, 15 pages.

Beahm, William M. *The Meaning of Baptism.* Elgin: The Brethren Press, 8 pages.

Bowman, Warren D. *Anointing for Healing.* Elgin: The Brethren Press, 1942, 25 pages.

Brumbaugh, M.G. *History of the Brethren.* Elgin: Brethren Publishing House, 1906, 559 pages.

Eller, Vernard. *In Place of Sacraments, A Study of Baptism and the Lord's Supper,* Grand Rapids: Eerdmans, 1972, 144 pages.

Kurtz, D.W. *The Teaching of the Symbols.* Elgin: Church of the Brethren General Mission Board, 1931, 16 pages.

Chapter 6
1. Read the following Bible passages, noting especially the emphasis placed on lay responsibility in worship: Deut. 26:1-11

(lay obligations in bringing an offering); 1 Cor. 14:26 (lay contributions to public worship); Eph. 4:7, 11-16 (distribution of gifts to laypersons); and 1 Peter 2:5-9 (the priesthood of all God's people).

2. Another text, underscoring the importance of unity within the community as a basis for worship, is Rom. 25:5-6. Consider the "togetherness" aspect of Brethren church assemblies either as you recall them or as you may have read about them. Are there dangers as well as positive values in celebrating the family aspects? Do church members, in your opinion, have a vision of belonging to more than a local assembly? Do their worship patterns reach out to encompass people who are "different"?

3. Take time to describe a recent Sunday worship service in your congregation. At what points does it resemble the activities of Brethren in the 1700's (page 64) or in the 1800's (page 65)?

4. On a sheet of paper draw a continuum (a line from left to right) for each of the five illustrations in the chapter under the topic, "Some Things Have Changed." For example, think of the meetinghouse at one end of the line, a church sanctuary at the other. Decide where your place of worship comes on that line, closer to the meetinghouse or to the sanctuary. Decide where you, personally, think it ought to be. Do the same for the other "things that have changed" in Brethren worship.

Durnbaugh, Donald F., editor. *The Church of the Brethren Past and Present*. Elgin: The Brethren Press, 1971 (especially chapter 4).

Fisher, Nevin W. *The History of Brethren Hymnbooks*. Bridgewater: Beacon, 1950, 153 pages.

Holsinger, Henry R. *History of the Tunkers and the Brethren Church*. 1901 (especially chapter 9).

Lehman, James. *The Old Brethren*. Elgin: The Brethren Press, 1976, 384 pages (especially chapter 4).

Chapter 7

1. Read carefully the Bible passages (Eph. 5:15-20); Psalm 90:1-4, 9-12, 14-15; Eccles. 3:1-8; Romans 14:5-10; and Mark 2:23—3:4) that serve as guidelines for scheduling special worship occasions. Do they make a case for having a "Christian calendar"?

2. Look at your own church calendar (also, if available, the

outline of the church year in *The Brethren Reminder,* or the *Brethren Program Calendar.*) Decide to what extent it is traditional in view of the Christian Year and to what extent it is promotional for other activities.

3. Make a list of your own favorite times or seasons, including not only religious observances but other special events. How does your "personal year" overlap with your church's "Christian year"?

4. The old medieval calendar provided many special saint's days. But later church leaders wanted to include "all saints" and "all souls," so they planned festival days to include all that were not so special. Can you think of several "saints" or "souls"— particular Christians you would like to honor?

5. Many Sunday worship bulletins use themes from lectionary readings for each Sunday. Do the themes your bulletins show seem relevant to you as well as proper for the season?

Cowie, L.W., and Gummer, John Selwyn. *The Christian Calendar.* Springfield, Mass.: G. & C. Merriam Company, 1974, 256 pages.

Gibson, George M. *The Story of the Christian Year.* New York: Abingdon-Cokesbury, 1940, 238 pages.

Vipont, Elfrida. *Some Christian Festivals.* New York: Roy Publishers, 1963, 194 pages.

Chapter 8
1. Read Psalm 119:105-112 (a portion of an Old Testament tribute to the law as "word," "precept," "ordinance," "testimony," and "statute") and John 1:1-18 (a New Testament tribute to the eternal Word that became incarnate in Jesus "full of grace and truth"). Is it possible to distinguish the words of the scriptures from the word that God spoke in Christ?

2. Look at Psalm 90 in any translation already familiar to you. Try changing the words like "thou," "thee," "thy," "ye," to "you" and "your," also words like "hast," "hadst," "sayest," etc. to their modern equivalents. Does using your own language help in understanding? Is some sense of awe and mystery lost in the process? Try the same with a hymn such as "Come, Thou Almighty King."

3. Explore the section of your hymnal that offers verbal "Worship Aids" (pages 631-674 in *The Brethren Hymnal*). To what extent is the congregation involved in the actual reading of the words presented there? Think of ways such materials could be adapted or changed for new and fresh insights without

destroying their integrity—such as by writing paraphrases of some Bible readings, turning unison readings into antiphonal or responsive readings, or combining readings with hymn stanzas.

4. Make notes regarding one Sunday service in your church. Consider how the language in the service—Bible readings, words of hymns, prayers, sermon, etc.—would be understood by: an elderly couple who had grown up in the church, a young woman concerned about "sexist" language; a university professor who teaches literature; a factory worker who seldom reads; children under the age of twelve; and others who may prefer to hear familiar words but sometimes tire of them.

Emswiler, Sharon Neufer and Thomas Neufer. *Women and Worship, A Guide to Non-Sexist Hymns, Prayers, and Liturgies.* New York: Harper and Row, 1974, 115 pages.

Horn, Henry E. *Worship in Crisis.* Phila.: Fortress, 1972, 154 pages (especially chapters 5, 7 and 9).

Randolph, David James. *God's Party, A Guide to New Forms of Worship.* Nashville: Abingdon, 1975, 144 pages (especially chapters 4 and 5).

Russell, Letty M., editor. *The Liberating Word, A Guide to Nonsexist Interpretation of the Bible.* Phila.: Westminster Press, 1976, 121 pages.

White, James F. *New Forms of Worship.* New York: Abingdon, 1971, 222 pages (especially chapters 8 and 9).

Chapter 9

1. Read 2 Chron. 5:11-14 (music's part in the dedication of Solomon's temple); Psalm 150 (an invitation to praise God with singing, playing instruments and dancing); Isa. 6:1-8 (a vision associated with temple worship); Luke 2:14 (an angel song at Jesus' birth); Matt. 21:8-9 (a song of hosanna sung to Jesus); Mark 14:26 (singing the passover hymn at the Last Supper); Acts 16:25-27 (singing hymns in prison); 1 Cor. 14:7-19 (playing and singing to be understood); Col. 3:16-17 (singing thankfully); Eph. 5:15-20 (make music in your heart).

2. Become acquainted with your hymnal. Look at the various indices that show the source of biblical allusions, authors (what names do you recognize?), composers (are great works of music represented?), sources from folksongs and national anthems. How many hymns do you know well enough that you could sing at least one stanza from memory?

3. If your church uses worship bulletins, examine at least a

dozen of them to note how wide is the selection of hymns. Are just a few sung over and over? Are new ones ever introduced? Are responses from the hymnal ever sung by the congregation?

4. If your church choir sings anthems, ask the leaders to print the words so that you and other worshipers can read them while you listen. Are the texts well chosen? Does the music reflect the spirit and meaning of the words?

5. If you were helping to plan for a hymn festival in your church, what five hymns would you like to see included? Could you find information about them that would help others to appreciate them?

Bailey, Albert E. *The Gospel in Hymns.* New York: Scribners, 1950, 600 pages.

Lovelace, Austin and Rice, W.C. *Music and Worship in the Church.* New York: Abingdon Press, revised and enlarged 1976, 220 pages.

Northcott, Cecil. *Hymns in Christian Worship.* Richmond: John Knox Press, 1964, 83 pages.

Routley, Erik. *Hymns Today and Tomorrow.* New York: Nashville, Abingdon Press, 1964, 205 pages.

Chapter 10

1. Walk through your church building, noting especially in the sanctuary but also elsewhere any symbols that you can recognize. Some may appear in windows, others in carvings on furnishings, some in the form of the building itself.

2. Select one of the image words or phrases from your earlier study of the Bible that seems especially meaningful to you, such as the good shepherd, the bread of life, the light of the world, the garden, or the hand of God. Then take a Bible concordance and look up many of the ways in which the image word is used in the scriptures. Out of your investigation you may develop an outline that would be helpful in planning a worship service.

3. Examine two or three familiar hymns to see how verbal symbols are employed in the text. Some examples would be "The King of Love My Shepherd Is" or "When I Survey the Wondrous Cross."

4. Think of the most familiar rituals you observe in your church, such as the love feast and communion service. Consider to what extent these rituals are based on action symbols coming from the New Testament.

5. Visit a church that is more liturgical than your own and note the symbols used in the service and in the building.

6. As you think about symbolism, consider these questions: what symbols seem most in keeping with the Brethren heritage and emphases? At what point do symbols lose their suggestive value and become ends in themselves? Do you think that some of them become idols or graven images? In what helpful ways can today's symbols, symbols similar to some of the objects mentioned in the story that begins this chapter, be used effectively in worship services today?

Ferguson, George. *Signs and Symbols in Christian Art*. New York: Oxford University Press, 1954, 346 pages.

Miller, Joyce. *Christian Symbols*. Elgin, Ill.: Church of the Brethren General Board, 1975, 8 pages.

Miller, Madeleine S. *A Treasury of the Cross*. New York: Harper and Bro., 1956, 240 pages.

Rest, Friedrich. *Our Christian Symbols*. Philadelphia: Christian Education Press, 1954, 86 pages.

Snyder, Graydon. "Early Christian Symbols," *Messenger*. March 26, 1970.

Stafford, T.A. *Christian Symbolism in the Evangelical Churches*. New York: Abingdon Press, 1942, 176 pages.

Chapter 11

1. Read for yourself the sequence of Bible selections listed in the section, "Where God Dwells." As you follow the Hebrew experience with a stone, a tent, a tabernacle, a temple, and a synagogue, do you see steps in spiritual growth or do the places of meeting interfere with religion at its best? How do you feel about the hard words Jesus spoke regarding temple practices? In your opinion, what kind of church building seems best for the work and worship of the people of God?

2. Try to recall three of the worship experiences that have had the greatest influence in your life. How many were indoors, how many in some outdoor or temporary setting? To what extent did the place, the building or the immediate environment influence you?

3. Draw a floor plan of your church sanctuary. Decide what is the real focal center: an altar, a communion table, the pulpit, the organ or piano, the baptistry, the choir loft, or some designated worship center.

4. Sit quietly in your church sanctuary for ten minutes.

Then make notes of what the building says about God, about Jesus Christ, about the church fellowship, about the Bible, about ordinances and beliefs, about the church's outreach in service.

5. Make your own scrapbook of pictures of floor plans of church buildings, including historic churches or cathedrals you may visit as a tourist, but also of other churches similar to your own.

Bieler, Andre. *Architecture in Worship.* Philadelphia: The Westminster Press, 1965, 96 pages.

Sovik, E.A. *Architecture for Worship.* Minneapolis: Augsburg, 1973, 128 pages.

White, James F. *Protestant Worship and Church Architecture.* New York: Oxford Univ. Press.

Chapter 12

1. Read Ex. 35:30—39:43 (deliberate and detailed instructions for artists to create furnishings for the tabernacle, altar, veil, ark, basin, lampstand, and vestments for priests) and Deut. 4:15-31 (warnings against making graven images). Do these passages offer any positive as well as negative advice concerning the creation of an environment for worship?

2. Read Isa. 53 (a prophetic reference to the "suffering servant" usually identified with Christ) and 2 Cor. 4:1-6 (God's glory revealed in the face of Christ). Think of three works of art, familiar to you' that portray Jesus; and consider to what extent each one reflects human or more-than-human qualities in its portrayal.

3. If it is convenient for you to visit an art museum (if not, consult illustrative catalogues for museums in your public library), make a simple survey to determine how many pieces of art deal with religion or biblical themes, also which periods in art history seems to have the most religious art.

4. Take a personal inventory of the "environment for worship" that your own home provides, noting books, records, drawings, pictures, bulletin covers, posters, hangings, glass, draperies, etc. Does the environment change only at Christmas or Easter? Have you explored the possibility of borrowing paintings from a lending library?

Dillenberger, Jane. *Style and Content in Christian Art.* New York: Abingdon, 1965, 240 pages. 82 plates.

Maus, Cynthia Pearl. *Christ and the Fine Arts.* New York: Harper and Bro., 1938, 764 pages.

Newton, Eric and Neil, William. *2000 Years of Christian Art.* New York: Harper and Row, 1966, 318 pages.

Chapter 13

1. For a biblical example of innovation in worship that was probably well-intentioned but still created problems, read 2 Sam. 6:12-23. Can you appreciate King David's exuberant joy as he brought the ark to Jerusalem? Or do you feel as his wife did, that his actions were indecent? Is there a middle way in worship—between too many excesses and too many restraints?

2. Read 1 Cor. 12-14 to see how Paul dealt with a situation in which spontaneity in worship threatened to disrupt a congregation. Do you find guidelines here that can be helpful in evaluating or guiding the use of new worship patterns? Can a congregation be open to new forms of worship and still insure that "all things should be done decently and in order"?

3. If you were to represent the Church of the Brethren on a committee planning for an ecumenical worship service, what uniquely Brethren worship practices would you recommend to be experienced by others? Could you explain how they represent your own convictions regarding the nature of the church?

Bailey, Wilfred M. *Awakened Worship.* Nashville: Abingdon Press, 1972, 155 pages (especially Part III).

Christensen, James. *Contemporary Worship Services.* Old Tappan, Revell, 1971, 256 pages.

Christensen, James. *New Ways to Worship, More Contemporary Worship Services.* Old Tappan, Revell, 1973, 224 pages.

Hovda, Robert W., and Huck, Gabe. *There's No Place Like People, Planning Small Group Liturgies.* Chicago: Argus Communications, 1959, 133 pages.

Randolph, David James. *God's Party, A Guide to New Forms of Worship.* Nashville: Abingdon, 1975, 144 pages (especially chapters 1 and 7).

Taylor, Margaret Fisk. *A Time to Dance, Symbolic Movement in Worship.* The Sharing Company, 1967, 1976, 180 pages.

Watkins, Keith. *Liturgies in a Time When Cities Burn.* New York: Abingdon, 1969, 176 pages.

Winward, S.F. *The Reformation of Our Worship.* Richmond: John Knox Press, 1965, 126 pages (especially chapter 5).

A Glossary of Terms

a cappella. Vocal music sung without accompaniment.

acolyte. An assistant to the leader in a worship service, usually a young person who lights and extinguishes candles but who may have other duties.

acoustics. The qualities of a room that determine how well sounds can be heard or transmitted.

acrostic. A type of poetry in which the first letters of each line may form a word or follow the letters of the alphabet. Some Hebrew psalms are acrostics built upon the twenty-two letters of the Hebrew alphabet.

Advent. The season of the Christian year looking forward to the coming of Christ, including the four Sundays immediately before Christmas.

agape. A term applied in the early church to the fellowship meal in the love feast and communion service. From a Greek word for love.

Agnus Dei. A Latin phrase meaning "lamb of God," used in an ancient hymn and in early Christian liturgies. Also refers to symbols and signs picturing Jesus as the Lamb of God. From John 1:29.

allegory. A story or poem in which events and characters may have figurative meanings different from the surface meaning of the story itself.

alleluia or *hallelujah.* An expression of praise meaning "Praise the Lord."

alpha and *omega.* First and last letters of the Greek alphabet, often used to signify the first and last, or the beginning and the end. Used as symbols of Jesus Christ. From Rev. 1:8.

altar. A term applied to the communion table, often regarded as the most sacred place in a church or temple. The word also refers to raised places where sacrifices and offerings were made to a god. In many churches the altar is treated as the center of worship.

amen. A word indicating support or approval, meaning "so be it," or "may it become true." May be spoken or sung as a conclusion to a prayer hymn or anthem.

anabaptist. A term given to Protestant groups opposing infant baptism and supporting believers' baptism.

Anglo-Catholic. Church of England members who emphasize the Catholic character of their tradition and who are generally regarded as "high church" in worship expressions.

Anno Domini. A Latin phrase meaning "in the year of the Lord." Abbreviated as A.D. and used in dating the years of the Christian era.

antiphonal. Alternate reading or singing of verses and sentences, by one group in response to another, or by a congregation in response to a leader.

apse. The semicircular space at the end, usually the eastern end or the chancel end, of a church. In ancient churches the location of the bishop's seat.

Ash Wednesday. The first day of Lent. The seventh Wednesday before Easter.

Ascension Day. A festival day in honor of Jesus' ascension, the fortieth day after Easter. From Acts 1:1-9.

atrium. The entrance hall or main room of a Roman house. In early Christian churches, modeled after Roman halls, the atrium was often a meeting or waiting room.

baptistry. The place in a church where baptism is administered. Where infant baptism is practiced the baptistry may contain a font, often near the entrance. For adult baptism the location of the baptistry may be a more prominent part of the front or chancel area.

basilica. An early type of Christian church resembling a Roman public hall, rectangular in shape with a central nave and side aisles and with a narthex or entrance room at one end, an apse at the other.

bidding prayer. A form of prayer including a series of petitions with suggestions to pray for specific persons or things, often with times of silence for private prayers.

blasphemy. Irreverent or profane speech about God or sacred things, spoken with contempt and abuse.

breviary. A book containing prescribed prayers to be said daily, used chiefly by Roman Catholics.

Byzantine. A word to designate art and architecture of a period between the fourth and fifteenth centuries, most evident in Orthodox churches marked by domes, round arches, and elaborate mosaics.

cadence. The rhythmic character of music and poetry, marked by a rising and falling sound.

call to worship. A scriptural invitation near the beginning of a worship service, either spoken by a leader or sung by a choir.

candelabrum. An ornamental candleholder with several branches for candles.

canon. An ecclesiastical rule or law, indicating what is accepted, recognized, or required. May refer to specific parts of the Roman mass. In music, a type of composition, similar to a round, that may be repeated by different voices. "Canonical hours" refer to periods of the day set aside for prayer and worship.

cantata. A choral composition including choruses, solos, recitations, and interludes often arranged in a dramatic way.

canticle. A nonmetrical song or hymn intended to be sung or chanted, similar to psalms but including other hymns or songs from the Bible.

cantor. The person who leads the singing of a congregation or choir. The soloist in a synagogue service.

catacomb. Underground place of assembly near to tombs and other burial places. Place of meeting for worship used by early Christians.

catechumen. Persons preparing for baptism and church membership. Worship services in the early church included the participation of catechumens in the early part of the service but not in the communion service.

cathedral. The principle church in a diocese, where a bishop resided. From the Latin word meaning "chair," referring to the bishop's chair.

catholic. A word meaning comprehensive or all-embracing. When used with a small letter, it refers to the universal Christian church. When capitalized it refers to the Roman church under the authority of the Pope.

censer. A vessel used for burning incense during a worship service. Incense is considered symbolic of the prayers of the saints. See Rev. 8:3-5.

chalice. A term for a large cup used in the communion service.

chancel. The area of a church, usually in the front, containing a communion table, pulpit, and reading desk.

chant. A way of singing or reciting a series of words on just one tone. Often used for psalms and canticles, occasionally for prayers. The most ancient form of choral music.

Chanukah or *Hanukkah.* The feast of lights, an eight-day Jewish holiday, falling in December, commemorating the rededication of the temple in Jerusalem after the victory of the Maccabees.

chapel. A small place of worship, often within a larger building, sometimes associated with a palace or school.

choir. In a church building, the place set aside for singers and clergy. With reference to persons, a group of singers in a church.

152 MOVE IN OUR MIDST

chorale. A simple hymn tune sung in unison by the congregation, developed in Lutheran churches in the sixteenth century.

collect. A short formal prayer addressed to God and containing a petition for the people offered in the name of Christ.

communion. A common name for the ordinance or sacrament of the bread and cup, observed by nearly all Christian groups. Other terms are "breaking of bread," the "cup of blessing," and "the Lord's table."

confession. In public worship the term may describe a declaration of faith or a general acknowledgement of sin.

consecrate. To set apart as holy or sacred, or to devote something to a specific purpose.

corporate worship. The experience of worship in which the church or a particular congregation participates as the body of Christ or the people of God.

counterpoint. A type of musical composition in which two or more melodies are interrelated and harmonized.

creed. A statement of faith summarizing the fundamental points of religious belief, often so written as to represent the views of a particular church.

cruciform. Shaped like a cross.

deacon. In liturgical churches, the principal assistant to the priest or celebrant. In other churches, a layperson who assists in duties not connected with preaching.

Deo gratias. Latin for "thanks be to God."

descant. An ornamental melody written above the soprano part to give brilliance to hymns.

diapason. The foundation tone of a pipe organ.

dissenter. One who refuses to conform to the rules and beliefs of an established church.

dorsal, or *dossal.* An ornamental cloth hung at the back of an altar or on a wall at the rear of the chancel.

doxology. A short formula expressing praise to God and mentioning the persons of the Trinity. Some churches use a doxology as a response after receiving an offering.

Epiphany. January 6, the twelfth day of Christmas, commemorating the visit of the Wise Men. From a Greek word meaning appearance, or manifestation.

epistle. A term for letters written by the apostles and appearing in the New Testament, from which selections are read regularly in many churches.

eucharist. A word meaning "thanksgiving," probably the most ancient name for the Lord's Supper, viewing holy communion as the great thanksgiving offered to Christians by God through Jesus Christ.

evensong. A church service said or sung in the late afternoon or evening, especially in the Church of England.

extemporaneous. A word to describe prayers or comments offered freely with or without notes, but usually not written out or committed to memory.

fetish. A material object supposed to have magical powers, often worshiped by primitive people.

font. A container for water used in baptism by sprinkling or pouring.

free church. A church that does not require a fixed ritual for its services. Such churches may have recommended orders of worship but allow freedom within that order.

fugue. A highly developed form of music composition in which three or four voices in turn take up a theme and develop it. Best examples are found in the organ music of J. S. Bach.

Gloria in Excelsis. Latin for "glory to God in the highest." An ancient hymn used in early communion services. From Luke 2:14.

Gloria Patri. Latin for "glory be to the Father," a doxology thought to be used originally as an ending to an Old Testament psalm, and still widely used in church services.

Gloria Tibi. Latin for "glory be to Thee," the beginning of a traditional doxology.

gospel. In the New Testament the gospel is the good news of salvation through Jesus Christ. In some worship services the term applies to a scripture reading from one of the four Gospels.

Gothic. A prominent type of church art and architecture developed in northern Europe in the Middle Ages. Chief characteristics are the pointed arch, vaulted roof, stained-glass windows, flying buttresses, spires, and pinnacles.

hallel. A Jewish ritual hymn of praise, consisting of Psalms 113 to 118, sung during holy days and festival seasons.

harmony. In music, a simultaneous combination of sounds developed in a single chord or succession of chords.

hosanna. A shout of praise to God, a cry of acclamation. From the Hebrew, meaning "save, we pray."

icon. A sacred picture or image of Christ or of one of the saints, reverenced by Eastern Orthodox churches for what they symbolize.

iconostasis. A huge screen, covered with icons, separating the sanctuary from the main part of Orthodox churches.

illumination. The art of decorating the texts of biblical manuscripts with colors and drawings, especially initial letters in rich colors and adorned with gold leaf.

immanence. The presence of God in God's creation.

incarnation. The embodiment of God in the person of Jesus Christ.

inner light. The light of Christ within the soul, serving as a spiritual guide, emphasized in Quaker worship.

introit. One or more verses from the psalms, sung in liturgical churches at the entrance of the clergy into the sanctuary as an act of preparation for the service.

invocation. A prayer at the beginning of a service calling upon God to be present and to bless the service.

Kaddish. A Hebrew prayer recited in the synagogue, especially at a time of mourning.

Kyrie Eleison. Greek for "Lord, have mercy upon us." A traditional response used in both eastern and western liturgies as a plea to God and as an act of praise.

lectern. The reading desk from which Bible passages are read. When churches have both a lectern and a pulpit, the sermon is usually given from the pulpit.

lectionary. A book listing scripture readings appointed to be read on all the Sundays and festivals of the church year.

Lent. The season from Ash Wednesday to Easter, forty weekdays observed as a time for repentance and fasting.

litany. A form of prayer in which the people offer fixed or similar responses to a series of petitions by a leader.

liturgy. A word that comes from Greek words meaning "the work of the people," referring to acts of public service. The New Testament concept would include the whole activity of the people in offering to God this "reasonable service" or "spiritual worship" (Rom. 12:1). In common use the word refers to ceremonies of the church and to certain specific liturgies that are precisely followed.

magnificat. An early Christian canticle, one of the nativity hymns included in Luke's Gospel (Luke 1:46-55).

mass. A word used by Roman Catholics and some Lutherans to describe the ceremonial services associated with Holy Communion. The name comes from the Latin words of dismissal "ite, missa est" meaning "Go, it is ended."

matins. In the Anglican church, morning prayers. In the Roman church, one of the daily offices, recited at midnight.

Maundy Thursday. The Thursday before Good Friday, a time commemorating Jesus' washing of the disciples' feet and the Lord's Supper.

meter, metrical. The number of syllables and their accents determine the meter of a line of poetry. In setting words to music the notes and rhythm of the music must match the meter of the verse. Metrical arrangements of the psalms are needed if the psalms are to be sung to fixed tunes. A metrical index in a hymnal is an aid to matching hymn texts with suitable tunes.

missal. A Roman Catholic service book for use in participating in the mass.

mitre. The ceremonial headdress of a bishop.

mosaic. Pictures and patterns made by cementing together small pieces of glass and stone. Used as ornamentation and illustration of biblical themes in Byzantine churches.

motet. A sacred choral composition usually based on biblical prose texts and sung without accompaniment.

narthex. A portico or vestibule on the western end of a church, divided by a wall or screen from the nave. In modern churches, an entrance room or vestibule.

nave. The central area of a church where most of the congregation are seated. From a Latin word meaning boat or ship.

nonconformist. A person who refuses to confrom to the requirements of an established church.

Nunc Dimittis. An early Christian canticle, one of the nativity hymns included in Luke's Gospel, the song of Simeon (Luke 2:29).

offertory. A hymn, prayer, anthem, or instrumental piece sung or played during the gathering of the offering. In some services, the "offering" refers specifically to the bringing of bread and wine for the communion service.

office. In reference to worship, the word may describe the order of a liturgical service or it may apply to parts of the service such as those led by a choir.

oratorio. A musical composition based on a dramatic text or poem, with arias and choruses, with orchestral accompaniment, but without action or scenery.

ordinance. An established religious ceremony explained as being ordained by God or ordered by biblical authority. In Brethren usage the usual sacraments are regarded as ordinances of the church.

orthodox. The word refers to correctness of teaching. It is a general name for Eastern churches which emphasize "the right giving of glory" to God.

Passover. An eight-day Jewish festival in March or April

commemorating the escape of the Hebrews from Egypt. (Exodus 12).

pax. Latin word for peace.

penance. Any act or punishment undertaken to show sorrow for sin or to obtain a pardon.

Pentecost. A Christian festival commemorating the coming of the Holy Spirit, observed on the fiftieth day after Easter.

peristyle. A row of columns surrounding a temple or a court, a colonnade.

phylactery. Small leather case containing texts from the Jewish law, worn by devout Jews during morning prayers (Matt. 23:5).

pietism. A movement in the church in Germany in the late 1600's emphasizing personal piety, Bible study, and works of charity. A strong influence on the beginnings of the Church of the Brethren.

plainsong. Unison choral singing of liturgical texts, melodic but unmeasured. Commonly used in the Middle Ages.

postlude. Concluding musical number in a service of worship, often played on organ or piano.

precentor. Leader of a choir or of congregational singing.

prelude. An instrumental musical number played just prior to the beginning of a worship service.

processional. A hymn or anthem sung at the opening of a service as participants move forward to take their places. It often symbolizes and assists the gathering of people for worship.

profanation. An act that shows contempt or disregard for something holy or sacred.

psalmody. The use of psalms or hymns in public worship.

psalter. The collection of psalms used in worship.

Purim. Jewish religious holiday commemorating the delivery of the Jews from being massacred by Haman (Esther 9:20-32).

recessional. A hymn or instrumental music used as choir and/or worship leaders leave the service.

recitative. A type of solo singing allowing liberty to the singer in interpreting a text, often used for scriptural texts in an oratorio or cantata.

relic. Something that remains from the past, especially some object belonging to or associated with an apostle or a saint and preserved as a sacred memorial.

reredos. The screen erected behind an altar, built of stone or carved from wood, often containing sculptured figures.

response. A part of a service in which a congregation sings or speaks in reply to a leader, or a choral response offered after scripture readings or prayers.

rite. A religious ceremony, act, or observance.

ritual. A word used to describe a prescribed order of service, or the content of a service, or a book setting forth the rites and ceremonies to be followed in a particular church.

Rogation Days. The Monday, Tuesday, and Wednesday before Ascension Day.

Romanesque. Style of architecture using round arches and vaults, in Europe during the early Middle Ages.

rood screen. A gallery built over the chancel in some churches in which stood a cross or "rood." Later, an ornamental screen that separated the nave and the choir.

Rosh Hashanah. The Jewish New Year.

rubric. Directions for the conduct of services. The name comes from red ink used for directions, in contrast to the black ink used for the text of services.

Sabbath. Day for rest and worship. The term is used primarily for the Jewish Sabbath (Saturday). Sunday is sometimes referred to as the Christian Sabbath.

sacrament. An act of worship, following the pattern or instruction of Jesus, using outward and visible symbols to represent what God is doing for persons, not what persons do for God. In Brethren usage a more common word is "ordinance."

salutation. An act of greeting. The term may refer to liturgical greetings that precede prayers and benedictions. Among Brethren the word usually indicates the holy kiss or embrace with which brothers and sisters greet one another.

sanctuary. A place of worship, as distinguished from a hall or auditorium. The word is usually applied to the entire meeting place for worship, but in some churches the term is reserved for the portion of the building that contains the altar or communion table.

Sanctus. Latin word for "holy," often used to designate the angelic hymn from Isa. 6:3 that is included in the Roman mass and in many other services.

Seder. Religious festival held in Jewish homes at the beginning of Passover.

Selah. A Hebrew word used frequently in the psalms, likely a musical direction, perhaps meaning, "Pause here."

separatist. One who withdraws or separates from a larger group, particularly one who opposes and withdraws from an established or state church.

Shema. The name given to the passage beginning "Hear, O Israel" (Deut. 6:4) recited by Jews as a confession of faith.

shofar. A musical instrument made from a curved ram's horn.

Shrove Tuesday. The day before Ash Wednesday. Last day before Lent. It is often a time of feasting just prior to the fasting observed during Lent.

spiritual. A sacred song or hymn as originally created by black or white worshipers in the southern United States.

stole. A long scarf or strip of cloth worn around the neck by ministers and choristers who are robed.

Succoth. A Jewish festival in the fall marked by the building of booths or temporary shelters (Lev. 23:33-34).

sursum corda. Latin for "Lift up your hearts." The response of the people is "We lift them up unto the Lord."

synagogue. Jewish assembly for worship and study. Also the building used for Jewish worship.

tabernacle. A worship center in a tent, used by Israelites before they had a temple. In Roman Catholic use, a receptacle for the "reserved sacrament."

Te Deum. Beginning words of a Latin hymn, "Te Deum Laudamus," meaning "We praise thee, O God."

timbrel. Ancient musical instrument, similar to a tambourine.

Torah. Hebrew word for law, usually applied to the first five books of the Old Testament, but may also refer to the whole body of Jewish religious literature.

transcendance. Aspects of God's character and presence above and beyond the physical universe.

transept. The sections of a Gothic church that extend out at right angles to the nave, forming the arms in the pattern of a cross.

transubstantiation. The Roman Catholic teaching that in the consecration of the elements in the mass, the bread and wine are changed into the substance of the body and blood of Christ.

trefoil. A plant with three leaves, used in designs as a symbol of the Trinity.

unison. Singing together in one part, following the melodic line. Reading together as with one voice.

vaulting. The arched roof or ceiling of churches, sometimes elaborately decorated.

verger. A church caretaker or usher. Or one who carries a symbolic rod or staff before a church official in a procession.

versicle. Short statements in a worship service usually followed by a congregational or choral response.

vespers. Late afternoon or evening service.

vestibule. Small entrance hall or room.

vestment. Robe, gown, or other special article of clothing worn by an officiant in a religious service.

vigil. A service of watching and praying on the eve of a holy day or festival.

Yom Kippur. Jewish fast day, called the day of atonement (Lev. 16:29-34).